THE LOST WAY

Book I

The Call

First published by O Books, 2008
O Books is an imprint of John Hunt Publishing Ltd., The Bothy, Deershot Lodge, Park Lane, Ropley,
Hants, SO24 0BE, UK
office1@o-books.net
www.o-books.net

Distribution in:	South Africa
	Alternative Books
UK and Europe	altbook@peterhyde.co.za
Orca Book Services	Tel: 021 555 4027 Fax: 021 447 1430
orders@orcabookservices.co.uk	
Tel: 01202 665432 Fax: 01202 666219	Text copyright A. R. McNeilage 2008
Int. code (44)	
	Design: Stuart Davies
USA and Canada	
NBN	ISBN: 978 1 84694 144 3
custserv@nbnbooks.com	
Tel: 1 800 462 6420 Fax: 1 800 338 4550	All rights reserved. Except for brief quotations
	in critical articles or reviews, no part of this
Australia and New Zealand	book may be reproduced in any manner without
Brumby Books	prior written permission from the publishers.
sales@brumbybooks.com.au	
Tel: 61 3 9761 5535 Fax: 61 3 9761 7095	The rights of A. R. McNeilage as author have
	been asserted in accordance with the
Far East (offices in Singapore, Thailand,	Copyright, Designs and Patents Act 1988.
Hong Kong, Taiwan)	
Pansing Distribution Pte Ltd	
kemal@pansing.com	A CIP catalogue record for this book is available
Tel: 65 6319 9939 Fax: 65 6462 5761	from the British Library.

Printed by Digital Book Print

THE LOST WAY

Book I
The Call

A. R. McNeilage

BOOKS

Winchester, UK
Washington, USA

CONTENTS

Silence is praise

PREFACE

Christianity is a way of Love. Everything existing arises from Love, is permeated and maintained by Love and will return to the Source of Love - to God.

To learn to know that we are Love - however remote that idea might seem to us, here, now - is what is asked of us. It is the most terrible command of all. It leads us from the safety of mental captivity and illusion towards our fear of the freedom and the truth we long for in our souls.

God's Love is an eternal call from above. To receive this everlasting invitation to return home was, is now and will be forevermore, the only true aim of our existence.

The love of the Son for the Father and the power of Holy Spirit all guide us to the vastness of Love, to which we belong, and teach us that we are not separate, as we seem.

Nothing is more important than this for us, for our neighbors, for the world and for God. How can we open to holiness in all aspects of our lives? The task and responsibility of a Christian is to allow ourselves to be moved ever closer, towards the Everlasting.

Jesus of Nazareth, Yeshua bar Alaha, Jesus, Son of God, taught this way of the heart 2000 years ago. What remain are the teachings of the Gospels, which extol us to become Christians, but the means necessary to succeed has been lost.

Today, faith has become blind, hope has become cowardice and love has become need. We betray the spirit of Christ in ourselves every day. We must stop believing in God and start trying to experience his existence within ourselves. We must take back personal responsibility for moving towards a new inner relationship with the Infinite. We have to start asking questions of ourselves and stop assuming we know.

True Christianity involves an inner practice of the heart to establish grace, harmony and love in our daily lives. To rediscover the Christian heart demands an exact method. I cannot think myself into becoming a Christian. Our aim is to open our hearts and, through them, be guided by God's Love.

To strive to become Christian is the greatest of all endeavors. It leads us away from the fear of death to the joy and the bliss of true relationship with the Everlasting - communion in the service of the Lord.

Is it possible to establish our own wish to deeply experience a relationship with God? Perhaps all we have available to us is the chance to see how far away we are now and, more and more, through that sensitive awareness, to change our state to one of greater openness and receptivity. In this state there is something new to be understood; something that is true and free. We can experience the influence of this new understanding through our hearts alone.

We can also feel the joy of a heart infused by a love and stillness that opens us to other people's suffering and to a new trust. Our hearts break open to the infinite unity of the soul. Then we enter a relationship where it is not that *I see* but *I am seen*.

We could never be further from God yet, at the same time, He could never be closer to us than He is now... than He is always.

For those of us who *feel* the truth of what is written here, may it bring new life to our struggle to become Christian. To those of us who fear and reject what we read, here, throw away this book. Do not let it disturb you. You are the lucky ones. For you, life can continue as before. You will not have to give up your dreams of what will make you happy.

This gospel of knowledge, written as it has been in such strange circumstances, does not offer the comfort of beliefs, only the injunction to remain in living question, willing to confront the mystery of God's loving presence. It is a faithful transmission of the teaching, which the disciples received directly from Jesus. It demanded then - and it demands of us now – the challenge of an energetic Christian practice in the immediacy of the present moment.

In some extraordinary way this teaching has been given to us as vibrant and lucid in the 21st century as if Jesus of Nazareth had spoken the words today. And who will listen? All are called yet few respond. Am I open to this holy summons?

INTRODUCTION

The story of this gospel and how it came to be written is an extraordinary one. I scarcely believe it myself...yet, in many ways, the author of the knowledge offered here is the least important aspect of the book.

The understanding in these pages is to be questioned, explored, treated with curiosity and tested through our own experience. All that we have available to us to receive the living energy of God is the heart of our soul, which resides in eternity within our own bodies. All our actions, whether we realize it or not, serve to further us in a living exploration of what that means.

My involvement began on June 1st 2005 when my brother called from Jerusalem. We hadn't been in contact for several months and I wasn't even aware he had left the country.

I don't want to share a great deal about my brother but let me just say that I love him very much. Hugh is five years older than I am. Our mother died when I was six and our father died in an accident when I was 15. Hugh's solid, warm presence took away much of the pain of that experience and his love and care and support never flinched through all the times I made it difficult for him.

It was 3.20 in the morning and the sound of the telephone shocked me awake from a deep sleep.

"Rob? It's Hugh. Listen. I'm going to be arriving at Heathrow later today with a friend who is rather ill and I need a lift back to the farm. Could you meet us?"

That was how it began. I remember I was irritated that

he expected me to drop everything at such short notice.

He asked me to repeat the arrival time and flight number and suggested I hire something bigger and more comfortable than my own car.

Later that morning, I glided into the short stay car park of Terminal 4 at the wheel of a dark blue Mercedes in time to meet the 11.40 BA flight from Tel Aviv. I parked on the ground floor across from the terminal and as near the arrivals gate as I could get.

Hugh appeared pushing a figure in a wheelchair. My brother looked tanned, healthy and full of vigor. He smiled broadly when he saw me. By contrast, the hunched body of what I assumed to be a man sat bent forward in the chair. He was dressed in dark tracksuit bottoms and a thick red sweatshirt with the hood drawn over his head. He wore dark glasses against the light and the wires from a CD Walkman in his lap trailed upwards to both ears, hidden deep in the recesses of the hood.

Hugh hugged me to him and then, with his big hands still gripping me by my shoulders, held me at a distance so that he could focus on my face. He eyed me closely and, apparently satisfied by the results of his examination, hugged me again.

He made no attempt to introduce me to his friend. I led them both to where the car was parked, pushing their luggage on a trolley. By the time I had put the cases in the boot, Hugh had managed to maneuver the body from the chair onto the back seat of the car. A porter took the wheelchair and left.

Before getting in himself, Hugh signaled to me to stay outside the car a moment and we spoke across the roof.

"Peter is extremely sensitive to the energetic disturbance of negative emotions. I don't want to talk while we are in the car. I know that might be difficult but we will have time once we're home for me to explain what all this is about."

He laughed at my expression. I was always full of questions and it was no surprise to him that I had become a journalist. He knew exactly how much I would hate having to remain in suspense.

"What would be most useful would be to focus as much as possible on our loving feelings for each other or for people we regard as special in our lives.

"Anxiety, fear and anger are incredibly painful to Peter, just at the moment, so try to notice if those come when you're driving and think of something as an antidote to them as quickly as possible. Allow memories of happiness and times and places and events when you felt most peaceful – staying calm would be better than excitement. Try to avoid your usual impatience on the journey home. We have all the time we need so don't rush.

"I'm sorry to put you through this but all I can say is he deserves our consideration. The world will have reason to be incredibly grateful to Peter."

We drove in silence and I have to admit I felt tense and anxious as I struggled to "think happy" while worrying about the onset of irritation and frustration at our slow progress. Fortunately, the traffic on the M25 motorway was lighter than usual and we reached the M11 without too many delays.

My attention was constantly drawn to the figure in the back. He sat motionless most of the time. Occasionally he would look out of the window at the rolling countryside sweeping past.

Hugh would turn and smile from time to time. He looked tired now and several times his head dropped before he forced himself awake again. In less than an hour both of them were fast asleep and I relaxed a little.

East Anglia was home to Hugh and me. After our

mother died, our father had been a vicar in Great Dunmow for most of our childhood before moving to Braintree, and our summers had been spent on the coast at Aldeburgh with our grandmother. We turned brown in the Suffolk sun and wind as we explored the muddy creaks of the River Orr in our little gaff-rigged dinghy.

The expanding skies greeted me again as I drove north from London. I turned off at the Stansted Airport junction onto the A120 and woke Hugh for directions for the rest of the way.

He had been living in a community for the last ten years but I had never been invited. We had always met in London. It didn't bother me much. Some of his friends could be a bit strange and I imagined feeling quite uncomfortable around them.

The farmhouse, Hugh told me, was empty and we would be alone. I followed his instructions through Thaxted and Great Bardfield. We wound our way down narrow lanes past fields of green wheat, and pale pink and white dog roses in full bloom amongst the hedgerows of blackthorn blossom and cream elder flowers.

The farm lay at the end of a long single-track lane sheltered in the folds of three gentle hills. It was an old Essex Farm house with pan-tiled roof and small windows set in white, weather-boarded walls. It looked well kept and cared for.

Hugh leant round to face his friend. "We're here".

The figure in the back began to sob quietly. There was no explanation from Hugh. I stopped in the drive. Hugh touched my arm.

"I just need to think about this for a moment".

I waited in silence until he spoke again.

"If you can drive up as close as you can to the front door, I think Peter will be able to walk that far with my help. It's probably best if you don't touch him. Nothing personal. Here's the key. If you go through the hall, there is a white door on the left at the far end. If you could go in and close the curtains I can put him on the couch in there for now.

"I will need to stay with him until well after dark. As more people sleep, the anxiety levels fall and Peter will be able to rest without me. We can talk then. Make yourself at home. Maybe later you could go into town and get some fresh food – salad things, fish but no meat, vegetables and any kind of soya products...fruit, too, would be good and milk...you'll see what to buy when you get there. There's a brown tin in the right hand drawer of the dresser in the kitchen. There should be enough money in it for the shopping".

I found the door and was just leaving the darkened room as Hugh arrived, supporting Peter. I held the door open and waited until my brother had struggled to the couch with the limp body. The hood of the sweatshirt had fallen back to reveal a shaven head and incredibly white, almost bloodless skin.

Hugh registered my curiosity with a smile, signaled me to withdraw and closed the door, leaving me alone in the hall.

I wandered about the house. Some of the doors upstairs were locked but there were two large bedrooms with vaulted ceilings that had been turned into dormitories by the addition of bunk beds. Downstairs, apart from the room that Hugh and Peter occupied and the kitchen, there were three other large rooms. One was the dining room with a long refectory table taking up most of the space. The other was a lounge with comfortable sofas and armchairs and shelving, packed with books, taking up most of one wall. They contained well-ordered sections on Christianity, Buddhism, Hinduism, Sufism, Islam, Judaism and other collections of spiritual works including Krishnamurti, Gurdjieff and Ramana Maharshi.

The other room was simple and bare except for a number of meditation stools arranged in a circle on a large Persian carpet. The walls were bare but for one simple wooden cross, made from two stripped branches of what looked like oak. All I can say is that its effect on me was striking and powerful and grew even more so as my stay at the farm went by.

I was asleep on the sofa when Hugh woke me. It was nearly midnight. He turned on a lamp and handed me a coffee. I had expected him to be tired, like me, but he seemed light and rested and there was a quiet energy almost radiating from him.

As we sat enveloped by the yellow lamplight and by the deeper silence of the countryside, he laughed to himself at the strangeness of what he was about to say and began to recount the extraordinary story of what had happened to him and his friends.

A few people had come and gone over time but for the most part, Hugh and nine others had been at the farm for the last eight years. They had gathered together by strange chance, word of mouth and by any of the other mysterious coincidences that can lead people to a particular spiritual path.

They formed what they called a study group to explore "deep" Christianity. Hugh explained that, to them, this had meant a contemplative path of meditation and practical study of Gnosticism, esoteric Christian texts and the ancient knowledge upon which Jesus had based his teaching.

"Most of us had some kind of income and the rent was extremely low. By pooling our money we managed to live perfectly comfortably. We grew what vegetables we could and we had chickens and geese.

"Peter, the man who was to become our master, arrived five years to the day after we had moved here. We received a letter from solicitors to say that the owner of the house wanted to stay for a short while on retreat and wished to know if he would be welcome. What could we say? We knew he must be sympathetic to what we were doing because we had been clear about it when we signed the lease. Yet we had never met our landlord and knew nothing about him.

"Some of us were more suspicious than others but none of us knew what to expect. We wrote back to ask how long he wished to stay. Instead of a reply, we heard a knock at the door one morning and there he was.

"He was the opposite of how you saw him today - strong, erect and with shining blue eyes that pierced you to the soul. His face exuded a kindness that grew to love as you watched it.

"He announced who he was at the door and that he would stay a short time. That was all he said. He introduced himself to the rest of us when we gathered for lunch and he didn't speak again for nearly four months. Yes! He never left after his arrival. During that time, whatever we asked him to do, he would do without question and with the same expression of kindness and warmth towards us.

"He became like a servant. His silence, though, affected all of us. We began to talk less ourselves and a new atmosphere began to settle around the house. We began to do things more quietly. There was more mindfulness in what we did.

"You could tell when he entered a room, even if you weren't looking. A different quality of silence permeated the space and it was tangible. We began to go deeper within ourselves.

"He first spoke to us properly in his capacity as our

spiritual master on the 7th of September 2001. We had noticed a change in him during the previous week. Something more imperative about him began to appear, along with a certain heaviness and sadness. By now we were all particularly sensitive and attuned to his presence and we noticed not quite an agitation but it was clear that something was causing him very deep suffering.

"In the silence which now followed our morning meditation together, he told us that in four days time man's growing separation from God would be made visible. Some powerful act of hatred and ignorance would happen in America. He said the inner war, which came from that separateness, would also be made visible in a new armed conflict. Fear, which already existed throughout the world in a terrifying way, would spread ever deeper into our hearts and our relationship to the oneness of the Infinite would weaken even more. God's action upon the world through mankind was in danger of ebbing away to the point where the Christian word would no longer exist as a living experience."

Hugh stopped. It was one o'clock in the morning. The darkness seemed to draw in upon us even more and the silence was thick and undisturbed until he spoke again.

"When 9/11 took place, it created in our master an intense holy suffering. He felt just how much Man had lost the presence of God within himself and he wept in his room. We could kill because we felt so separate from everyone else. We could kill in the name of God because we had become estranged from the true God. We had lost our link to the Everlasting. The pain of that terrible separation leads to chaos, as we contract our lives into a limited mental world. We needed, he said, to re-establish a living relationship and find a new way to conduct our lives with 'trust' in the Oneness to which we all belong.

"Our master said that we have to learn, as Christians, to live more fully in ourselves so that we can live more fully in the world. Our exile from the divine presence leaves us in fear of death and all our impulses and actions come from this fear.

"All that arises in the world is sacred, holy and wise. These qualities permeate all living things but we, in our isolation, cannot contact them. Even ugliness, sorrow and pain are part of that natural order – in their own way each contains the will of God. They are woven into the fabric of our existence as we are woven into every other thread of life. We cannot be separated.

"Only our reconnection to God can free us from the influence of fear. Were we to stop fighting life, we could accept its sacredness and the holiness of suffering. As Christians, we cannot change the world but we can change ourselves and open to the world as it is. Then the grace and gentleness of God can be here. We can allow God's love to come through us; more of it can be, and needs to be, felt in the world.

"God is not able to abandon us but we are in danger of abandoning him in such great numbers that the world will not be able to evolve as it could. That is also why I asked you to come."

If I'm honest, I didn't truly understand all that Hugh was saying and I laughed: "You want me to help you save the world!"

Hugh smiled: "Life has its own holy intelligence and there is nothing we can do to interfere. The world is always in prayer. Prayer exists as a sacred impulse in all things. Our own lives get confused by desire but true prayer, the prayer that is always in us, is like a river that never ceases to flow back towards the infinite ocean of its ultimate source.

"Our suffering is that we do not hear the ocean's call in us: that is why I want you to help me publish this holy text I'm about to put before you. It was written by a disciple of Jesus, I have no doubt about that.

"He has left behind a sacred text based on the first eight beatitudes of the Sermon on the Mount. A sermon he heard from Jesus' own lips. Our master told us that everything we needed to transform our practice was contained in these first eight beatitudes; and that the Sermon offered the path that led to the complete teaching of Jesus.

He must have seen my expression.

"For now, it is not important that you believe any of this", he said quickly.

"You have not experienced what we have experienced with him. He taught us that the aim of every Christian is to struggle to rest in the current of God's love and, by doing so, to allow God, through us, to have an action upon the world. In this lies the true meaning of 'to spread the word of God'.

"The purpose of a Christian is to serve God in this way but the Way is not easy. All our effort has to focus on opening the heart in order to return to God: the heart alone leads us to our resurrection.

"All that lies against us is the world created and maintained by the mind of the ego. It obscures our openness and through our own self-seeking and self-building it opposes our search for the Lord. This Christian struggle takes place in every moment as we open to presence - the presence of God's Love in us.

"The heart alone is capable of understanding what the mind and its words can only point to. How is this to be done? All the instructions necessary are contained in the Sermon.

"We found that they included all we needed to energize

and bring alive our Christian practice. We began to engage in a newly-invigorated struggle and to feel again the joy of being on a true Christian path. This immediate form of living Christianity gave us new meaning and purpose. It opened our eyes to a new way of living – a way of living that gave us direct experience of Jesus' teaching to his disciples.

"It is a teaching that had become lost. This gospel written by our master restores it to us at a time in our history when it is most desperately needed. I want you to bring it to public awareness. Read it."

He handed me five typewritten sheets of foolscap paper.

CHAPTER I

The Gospel in its Original Form

Blessed are the poor in spirit: for theirs is the kingdom of heaven. *God is Love. All that is between us is Love. When all else ends, what remains is Love. I must open my heart as completely as I can so that any self-desire is burnt away by this Love. When I am helpless before God, then, through me, God becomes great and, through him, I become nothing; we become One. When "me" no longer commands and "I" no longer exists, then I am finally poor in spirit.*

True Christian practice opens me to love and real Love brings humility. The letting go of all self is the Christian path of Heart, when the divine light that is held captive in us ceases to appear separate and we are raised again to the Kingdom of Heaven, for Love's sake.

I search not in order to find but to participate on the Way. The path is the result. Nothing is to be sought but the understanding that we are the instruments of Divine Love. That Love permeates us all and, through it, I submit to the will of the Everlasting. The flames of Divine Love do not allow any part of the small self to cross the abyss that divides us from the kingdom of God. We must sacrifice the life of the self and trust in our own perfect goodness and wisdom. It becomes a holy battle between the heart and the mind.

To be a true Christian is to strive to remain in the fire of that

Divine Love and become poor in spirit. In this way I remain humble before God. I submit my will to His. Blessed are they without will. Only in the silence beyond self-will, in this state of poor in spirit, can I open to the Kingdom of Heaven. Thus do I surrender myself to the Will of God and to His reign in me.

Jesus, the Nazarene, taught me this.

Lord Have Mercy.

Blessed are they that mourn: for they shall be comforted. *We are permeated by God's Love all the time yet we do not feel it. I am called and do not hear. His Love is a force that flows through every living thing and it finds its highest expression on earth when we know it in our selves. Only in this way can we ease the suffering of our Lord.*

To mourn is a holy state of sorrow that God's Love is obscured in me. This is the beginning of the road towards Holy Desire; the beginning of longing for God, and the movement from my separate mind to the true feelings of the heart, which lead me to union.

I am far from home and alone. I mourn all that obstructs and diverts me from experiencing the love of God – that, too, is God's will. Lord give me the strength to suffer the mystery of your Will.

Let the fact that I do not devote all my attention to the presence of God in me be a source of deep sorrow. May I bear that struggle with resignation, patience and gratitude, and use it to feel God's Love, which is to praise the Lord.

God's Will is that my heart is closed to Him. God's grace is that my heart opens in suffering to him. Here, now, I am in the mystery of what it is to be human and, in that remorse, I find the obedience to serve. Only through mourning can I ask for the grace that will allow my heart to listen and to receive from the Vastness that which will make me free.

Jesus, the Nazarene, taught me this.

Lord Have Mercy.

Blessed are the meek: for they shall inherit the earth. The world is known by those who turn away from it. To bring my gaze back within myself is to experience all the forces of the universe and to know God in me. To be meek is to let go of all that I wish for myself and simply experience how I am in the immediacy of the present without judgement. Through a deep acceptance I allow my inner life to be lived in me by the Divine Will. If I try to change what is, I immediately lose the help of Holy Spirit. By imposing my own wish, I refuse free passage to God's Will. I am lost in a world of reaction where I serve a lesser God of my own invention who bends to my difficulties and whose will I obey only on my own terms - a false God who accepts duality.

How do I notice my state without the "violence" of a wish to change it? To look in the mirror of my life is to see what is, without imposing how I wish it to be: All that has happened, all that is happening and all that is still to happen comes from God.

In meekness I can experience the Divine Presence. Away from self-desire and self-aversion, in silence and stillness I can open to the mystery of God's Love – a mystery that exists in me and in everything.

So in meekness I allow God to take up my effort, to guide the gathering of my awareness so that I can receive Him in my body. I open to the heart of Christian practice – to accept that, without God's grace, I cannot receive all that is my birthright. When the Lord wills it, I turn my attention inside to find Him ever waiting.

Jesus, the Nazarene taught me this.

Lord Have Mercy.

Blessed are they which do hunger and thirst after righteousness: for they shall be filled. My longing to return must burn within me. In the gathering and dispersal of my attention I see the tide of God's purpose. I rise and fall, hungering and thirsting, upon this ocean of Divine Will, as I wait to be filled by

Holy Spirit.

How close am I to the Divine? To know where God is in the life of my heart is my practice as a Christian, first and foremost, in every moment of my life. How open or closed am I to God's Love in the immediate present? Besides this constant enquiry, nothing else matters. This is the first step and the last step and the everlasting step towards God. I must learn to long for the Infinite and to transcend the mind that holds me back by submitting to the Holy pain of hungering and thirsting for all that God desires for me.

How do I find my way home? Raising my eyes to the Lord sets me free from the world of the mind, of flesh and matter. In my search for my own immediate Christian experience, I have to return to myself, again and again; to bring my awareness into my body to where I am; to change my state from forgetfulness to one of remembrance. I repeat this every moment by coming back to awareness. My aim is always to see how I am; the state of things in me...how far I am from God and how I can begin to open once more to infinite Oneness. My heart, like that of the Son, must break from longing to be with the Everlasting. I listen, always and forever, to the summons from Holy Spirit that reveals God in everything. I hunger and thirst for every moment, which offers me the gift of Christian renewal.

Jesus, the Nazarene, taught me this.

Lord Have Mercy.

Blessed are the merciful: for they shall obtain mercy. *We are the darkness through which God's light shines. Love needs my darkness to illuminate the presence of God. I submit to being loved. In building an earthly home for Divine Presence to enter into me, I am offering Love my mercy and, in return, my life receives the true gifts of Holy Spirit – the mercy of Divine Love and Holy Wisdom.*

The task of a Christian is to become a vessel for Love. I am filled with Holy Desire – not my own desire but the desire of God to express himself through me. My service is to open to Divine Will and, in doing so, I am opened to life.

As God is our beloved, so our souls are the beloved of God's Love. Through our souls' Holy Response, God knows himself.

I bring my heart to be filled with Christ's longing for the Everlasting. In that surrender, I offer my mercy. I am God's instrument when I live in humility and suffer His Will. All that I put before God is done in the name and spirit of Jesus Christ. In this way I rid my heart of the persecution of the self. I have to open myself to the influence of Holy Spirit as my guide in this. It floods its mercy, like water, into every place where love is obscured. Then my guilt and shame – the places in me that refuse to accept God's love - are transformed by new hope.

I feel God's mercy in the opening of my heart. To experience and accept this Law of Opening is to trust in the loving embrace of the Infinite.

Jesus, the Nazarene, taught me this.

Lord Have Mercy.

Blessed are the pure in heart: for they shall see God. *The only heart's desire God allows is the longing to be with Him. Even that, at the end, has to be renounced. Then I can be born anew in the light of the Lord's Divine Love. Accepting my death, I become, at last, alive.*

God can only be known by a heart that is empty of the needs of the self. It is a heart that has given up its wish to be free and happy. It loves for Love's sake and, through it, my soul returns in devotion to its source.

Divine Love leads me to be tested on the Cross of two worlds - this world and the next. To be aware of the touch of Divine Love is to be burnt by the Lord's command that the self cannot pass into the kingdom of God. In that moment, I am reminded and re-directed to the resurrection of our true purpose on earth. God's terrible resolve is to rid me of my self. Only then am I pure in heart.

I must abandon the arrogance of searching only for a connection to Heaven. I also belong to this world and the acceptance of both - of the whole of God's Will - is the essence of what it means to enter the place of pure in heart. Only this heart can witness and live Holy Truth.

The bridge between heaven and earth is Love. I have to let the divine illumination from above enter me. I allow myself to be led by the spirit of Christ, which, in the midst of my suffering reveals the Oneness behind all life and bids me sacrifice all that my self wishes to the bliss of everlasting Love. Through Jesus my heart opens to Holy Spirit and can once again hear the true voice of God...the voice of One that exists motionless behind all movement.

Jesus, the Nazarene, taught me this.

Lord Have Mercy.

Blessed are the peacemakers: for they shall be called the children of God. *To spread Silence is to spread the Word of God. To be in silence is to be touched by Holy Spirit. Without silence I cannot hear God in me nor see God in the simplicity and balance of nature and in all her wonders. In silence I am understood. In silence I am seen. In silence Love knows itself through me.*

Silence brings unity. When I belong to silence, I am no longer alone but part of the vastness of the Divine. Turning towards the direction of my source and resting in that stillness, I become again, for a moment, a child of God. My life and all that I am arises out of that silence, in the presence of God, as does everything existing.

All life is engaged in one spiritual journey of birth and death. By allowing life's flow to express itself through me, I see God's essence in all action. Through this innocence, I participate in the silent movement behind all life.

The peacemaker is born in silence from a birthplace in Love.

Listening in that silence, I free the world from my self.
    Jesus, the Nazarene, taught me this.
    Lord Have Mercy.

**Blessed are they which are persecuted for righteousness'
sake: for theirs is the kingdom of heaven.** *I cannot see God in
others until I see Him in myself. I cannot see love and forgiveness
in others until I know them in myself. Through the darkness in
others I see my self more clearly. I am persecuted by all that takes
me away from God yet only through that persecution can I feel the
strength of my wish to return and the power of Christ's spirit in
me. And so I measure myself constantly against the strength of
what would obscure the Divine Presence in me.*

*If I move away from the suffering of others for fear of it
destroying my own happiness, I place myself in loneliness and
separation. To be persecuted is to suffer the distractions of the
outside world that break the silence through which I hear the call
in me of Christ's wish to return. Though I live on the cross of two
worlds, there is no choice but to return to God.*

*All that resists the Love of God is in me. If I turn to allow
myself to be persecuted by that, I meet in myself the suffering that
belongs to Man since time began on earth. Only then can I feel
love's movement in me. If I persecute others, I persecute God. I
submit, instead, to living the passion of Christ within me.*

*The justice of the Lord is not the same as the justice of man. In
heaven there is only oneness: There is no punishment and reward,
no good or bad, no virtue or sin. There is a call in the silence to
Love and I must obey.*

    Jesus, the Nazarene, taught me this.
    Lord Have Mercy.

CHAPTER II

Holy Understanding

I put down the five pages and looked up at Hugh. I realized I had been reading a description of Christianity I had never encountered before. The "gospel" pointed to a new kind of Christianity that was full of energy and aliveness. It offered a path and a spiritual practice where one could make efforts to receive a direct experience of God's Love.

"You want me to get this published?"

"By itself, no. Each one of these beatitudes represents a lifetime of spiritual practice. They point the way but they are not *the* Way: that comes with all that our master had learned and experienced for himself with Jesus as *his* master and with what he transmitted to us...and, most importantly, what we put into practice."

"Are you telling me your master was one of the actual disciples?"

"Yes. The greatest of them."

"Which one?"

"I don't want you to know that. For now, I'm asking you to focus on the teachings he brought. Feel their impact in you. Later, you will understand."

He raised his hand to silence any more of my questions and smiled.

"To begin, then. The Way of a Christian, as our master

called it, is to loosen the grip of the mind and the emotions it produces – all of which separate us from God, from our fellow man and from nature - and to link to what we call 'Feelings', which can connect us again. The Christian task is to move away from the isolation of the ordinary egoistic mind towards a place where Feeling can exist in connection to the vast silence of the Kingdom of God, or the reign of God in us. In this way, we are released from 'hell'. This is the 'return' that is so often spoken about and it means a return to grace, harmony and love in our lives. All this is needed, if the world of Man is to evolve.

"Also, we found, that because they represent a complete teaching, every beatitude is woven like a thread within each of the others into a complete whole. Each one guards against the wrong perception of the practice associated with one before.

"I can pass on some of that knowledge to you and I thought that, as additional commentaries, they would be essential to impart some proper understanding of what to _do_ with the Gospel. It needs to become a new manual of Christian practice for those who recognize the summons from God that lies within it. It is not to come into the world as something to be believed. If it is to fulfill the role to which its author pointed, it must be experienced: only then can it be known as the Truth".

And so we began. It was easier than I had thought to take two weeks off at short notice and Hugh assured me that would be long enough. The pattern of those first few days left me alone during daylight and I would meet Hugh at midnight and work with him until about four in the morning. All I really needed at that stage was a tape recorder. He spoke so precisely that when the tapes were transcribed, the editing that was needed was negligible.

Each night we began with a new beatitude and the only

thing that interrupted his concentration and thought flow was my own curiosity about the man he called "master". He allowed these questions from time to time and, gradually, as I listened to him, I began to accept what had happened to my brother and his friends or "seekers of truth", as he called them.

In the deep quiet of the late night hours Hugh described his life with his master and laid before me a deep and profound Christian practice. He said that their master hardly ever referred to the Bible. He wanted everyone to begin where they were without preconceptions or prejudice; just an open, enquiring curiosity into "what is my state now and where is God in me?"

Hugh would make us both a hot drink before we started. He took a few sips, adjusted his chair in front of me so that we could see each other's faces in the lamplight and then signaled for me to begin reading aloud the Beatitude he wanted to talk about that night.

As I said, hardly any of what was subsequently transcribed from the tapes has been edited and it is reproduced in its entirety over the following eight chapters.

CHAPTER III

The Beatitudes

Hugh began my instruction by saying that the beatitudes came in an exact order and, according to his master, that was all that remained accurate in the Sermon described in Matthew's gospel.

"The First two beatitudes deal with how we should place ourselves before God. They refer to the movement away from separateness and ego to Oneness. They are instructions showing us how to live *as if* we were Christians and offer a way to place ourselves at the service of God's will. Without this inner attitude we have no hope of ever receiving Holy Spirit.

"The Second two beatitudes describe the guidance needed for our individual Christian practice: how we should approach our inner life and our struggle and effort to become more capable of being Christian. Through them, we can feel the re-energizing of our practice. We begin to open to God in a way that is truly miraculous and transforming.

"The Fifth and Sixth beatitudes deal with the deepening of practice and the necessity of coming alive to the soul as a bridge between heaven and earth. We are born to allow Divine Presence to have an action upon the world, through us, and we have to give ourselves up to that service. In return, we are freed from our suffering.

"The final two beatitudes deal with how we are to live in this world as Christians.

"Our master spent nearly four years with us studying and putting into practice this teaching. He stressed that what Jesus taught the masses was not the same as the teaching he gave to his close disciples.

"He said the beatitudes were a reminder to the disciples of all they had learnt from Jesus concerning their inner practice, before they moved out into the world. For us, today, they can act as a wonderful insight into the preparation that is needed to become Christian.

"The rigor of spiritual practice is a demand that comes through the instruction of the first eight beatitudes. These, and the Lord's Prayer, became our *living bible*.

"Our master hoped that this legacy would somehow re-energize Christian practice in the world today...something, he said, that in the light of recent world events, was more important than ever."

Author's note: In some of the chapters, I have highlighted sections in italics. These passages contain clarifications and explanations by Hugh in response to questions I asked, either during his talks or afterwards when I was transcribing the text from my recordings.

Hugh said that words like sin, hell, repentance, prayer, sacrifice, love, soul, salvation *and many others have to remain part of a constant questioning in us that establishes Christianity as a living search for God's Truth. For these words to be accepted mindlessly takes away aliveness and vigor from the struggle for the holy understanding that leads to Love. To believe we have reached a point where we know leaves Christianity barren and dead.*

He felt strongly that the teachings in this book needed to be read little by little. There are layers of meaning to be discovered and its sentences, paragraphs and pages need to be visited again and again so that more and more may be revealed.

CHAPTER IV

The Poor in Spirit

One

Blessed are the poor in spirit: for theirs is the kingdom of heaven.

God is Love. All that is between us is Love. When all else ends, what remains is Love. I must open my heart as completely as I can so that any self-desire is burnt away by this Love. When I am helpless before God, then, through me, God becomes great and, through him, I become nothing; we become One. When "me" no longer commands and "I" no longer exists, then I am finally poor in spirit.

True Christian practice opens me to love and real Love brings humility. The letting go of all self is the Christian path of Heart, when the divine light that is held captive in us ceases to appear separate and we are raised again to the Kingdom of Heaven, for Love's sake.

I search not in order to find but to participate on the Way. The path is the result. Nothing is to be sought but the understanding that we are the instruments of Divine Love. That Love permeates us all and, through it, I submit to the will of the Everlasting. The flames of Divine Love do not allow any part of the small self to cross the abyss that divides us from the kingdom of God. We must sacrifice the life of the self and trust in our own perfect goodness and wisdom. It becomes a holy battle between the heart and the mind.

To be a true Christian is to strive to remain in the fire of that Divine Love and become poor in spirit. In this way I remain humble before God. I submit my will to His. Blessed are they without will. Only in the silence beyond self-will, in this state of poor in spirit, can I open to the Kingdom of Heaven. Thus do I surrender myself to the Will of God and to His reign in me.

Jesus, the Nazarene, taught me this.

Lord Have Mercy.

One: Commentary

Hugh smiled when I finished reading this first beatitude. He paused for a long time and then began to speak.

"Our hearts long for Love; our minds turn us away from it. Hell, in the only true sense of the word, is the fear of being loved. Love sees all and we cover our faces from that look upon us; a look, which comes from above.

"The first beatitude sets out the task that faces us. We must struggle against the self by opening to Love. It is daunting and difficult and, without God's grace, impossible to achieve.

"The reality we face in our lives is that we are caught in these two forces of the heart and the mind. The mind leaves us separate from one another; the opening of the heart leads us together. The heart loves. The mind, in its fear, desires.

"The path of the Christian is very simple: it is to live in Love. God is Love. Therefore we have to learn how to experience Love in all things; how to experience the Divine Hand in all things. Eventually, we will directly experience His presence, as Love, in ourselves. For now, all we have, as aspiring Christians, is a wish to actively journey towards the Love of God in every moment of our lives.

"Of course we bandy around words like "love" and "god" without really knowing what they are. The path that our master showed us (the path that he himself was taught by Jesus) allows us to directly experience the power of Love within ourselves. Each time we are visited by this holy force, it burns away any sense of our own separateness and leaves us free of the self and 'poor in spirit'.

(Hugh said that Divine Love permeates all things, sustains all things in life. It is the energy behind all that exists. Everything comes from it and, ultimately, everything returns to the source of that Love.

We live, he said, in an ocean of Divine Love, a symphony of Divine Light, expressed through each of us as a single note. To know one note, one drop of the Divine, is to know the ocean. To know ourselves means to know God.

In all creation, nothing is separate yet in our darkness all we hear is our own individual note and not the greater music in us; all we feel is our loneliness. Our suffering and unhappiness lie in the blindness of our own minds.

According to Hugh, Love expresses itself as a natural response to all things. If we allow this process to proceed in us deeply enough, we will feel that we are God's Love. We will feel Oneness and a vast field of presence where we are not different but children of God and the same as every other living thing. The beatitudes guide us along this path).

"Christianity becomes a constant struggle to move away from a certain sense of separation to the gradual awakening and opening of the heart. Then we are led to God and to the Truth.

"To be poor in spirit is to be free of the forces of ego that deny us our heart's experience of the presence of God's Love. That means we have to put our rational mind in its proper place – not as a controlling and guiding force in our lives but as a servant to our task of always bearing God 'in mind'.

"The first beatitude is telling us that our aim is to open our hearts and be in the Love of God. We must let go of everything the ordinary mind wishes for; we have to begin by loosening its grip on our lives. The dilemma we face is that we are governed by our minds and *our minds cannot know God*. How do we learn to defy the desperate command of the self to know everything and, instead, trust in the mystery of God's will and purpose?

"This is what Jesus did. He taught his disciples the practical path of love that led them to give up their ordinary will in order to fully receive God's guiding Love.

"Whether we know it or not, we are all receivers of God's Love. Our purpose and our destiny are to consciously allow the Light of God to shine through us and, as a result, willed by the Absolute, for His Love to be able to act upon the world. Everything in life leads to that – even that which would take us away from understanding, ultimately leads us back to the truth of who we are. In fact, no force can stop us becoming Christian: it will happen, despite us, over a long period of our evolution or it can begin today with our participation when we strive to become poorer in spirit. God will wait for us forever. May His grace grant me patience.

"There is only one way in which we can open fully to the call from Above and that is to allow the dominating influence of the demands of the self to dissolve gently in what is real. We then lose the feeling of being so separate from everyone and have much more of a sense of 'being'. When we live our aim to become poor in spirit, we learn that the mind is blind and only the heart can see the truth of what we are... part of the vastness of the Infinite.

"I need to say, here, that it took a long time for any of this to happen. Our master's spirit and soul had been burnt pure by the love of Christ. Just to be in his presence had an enormous effect on our own inner states. His soul knew the freedom and bliss of the Kingdom of God and yet he was willing to be held captive once more in a human body. You cannot imagine the extent of the sacrifice involved in that act.

"He was willing to endure once again, directly, the pain of being human and, having tasted bliss, he must have felt that pain a thousand times more than we did. He loved us because we are all bound together in that pain. That is almost impossible to comprehend. He loved us because we, too, have the capacity to suffer for God's love. He thanked God with all his heart for being able to suffer afresh for us. The unimaginable suffering Christ bore and the suffering our master taught us to accept in ourselves is the holy suffering that guides us to God and to eternal bliss.

"When we gave up too quickly or took for granted what we were being given and stopped trying; when we were slow to understand, or when resistance made us appear lazy, you could almost feel this incredible sense of sorrow coming from him. Though he might scold or urge us on with a rebuke, we never felt his irritation or anger; rather there was this extraordinary impression of his love and his anguish. He was filled with an unbelievable compassion and you saw that, despite his holy task, and in the midst of his sorrow for us, he, too, trapped in a temporal nature, submitted to the will of God in all things. He would begin again with infinite patience and you felt in yourself the pain of his loneliness. Inwardly, at those times, I wept for him."

Hugh leant forward so his face was closer to me in order to emphasize what he was about to say.

"All our suffering points to God more clearly than any bible, if we but knew it.

"We do not realize that the feeling of missing something, of 'nothing is ever quite enough', is the echo of a holy desire to return to where we belong. Behind our outward search for happiness lies the longing of the soul for its real home.

"Empty of the one true relationship, we seek an antidote on the earthly plane through all that the mind thinks will make it happy. No thing, though, is ever enough. Blindly, the ego-self continues to look to the material world to comfort it and ignores the whispered secret of all those moments when the hearts of our souls are opened and we feel for a brief moment, the loving touch of our true home in the Infinite.

"The truth is that we can never be lost to God's love. Hunger for happiness is the seed of spiritual hunger – placed in us by God to dissolve the ego and bring us to the state of poor in spirit. This holy desire leads on to the longing-for-God-that-never-dies. All this is within us right now, waiting to be awakened.

"It's worth mentioning here that our master drew an important distinction between knowing and understanding. He said the mind could know but only the heart could understand.

("Mind" is another word that needs an explanation. Hugh said that there was a lower ego-mind that committed itself, through its fear, to the task of defending and maintaining our individual separate intention to exist as "me". There was, however, a higher mind that was governed by the heart and remained in its service. This higher mind was used to point towards the unknown and the unseen. It allowed itself to serve God. We live our lives through the ordinary mind: One creates suffering, the other serves holy understanding).

"On that day when our master first spoke to us, his words shattered the rule of our ego-minds. They had taken us to a place in ourselves where we had become safe and unquestioning in the comfortable habit of our practice. We had sought to find peace and contemplation by removing ourselves from the distractions of the world but all we had done was to remove what made our lives difficult and to avoid the forces against which we could measure the strength of our holy desire.

"Our master explained that Christianity guides us to our true relationship with the Oneness of God. To search for the truth of that Unity is to look without knowing and to wait without certainty. Only in this state when we are *poorer in spirit* can we open more to God's grace, and feel the breath of Holy Spirit upon us.

"Uncertainty moves us towards the divine. We have to sacrifice all the mind knows and open to the idea of it not knowing – the one thing the mind cannot bear. Our aim, through that, is to allow uncertainty to challenge what we have been taught to believe during the last 2000 years.

"The heart understands how to accept this journey but our hearts are closed, fearful of pain and hurt, defended against both judgement and its own feeling of vulnerability. The mind has employed the heart to defend its separateness. Yet there is another heart in us that knows – a heart that resides not in the mind but in the soul.

"This heart can transcend the power of the mind's concepts and illusions. We live now in a world that displays the highest examples of rational, scientific thought and yet we remain lost and wanting, searching ever more desperately for what in life has meaning. It is a world of separation and loneliness where the faint cry of the soul for union is heard only as a feeble summons that is soon lost and our search for happiness is once more diverted away from God to the immediate dramas of our lives. We cannot *think* ourselves into becoming Christians. We need to confront this in ourselves; to place an effort of our own in a different direction.

"From all that we were told by our master, Jesus was an incredibly down-to-earth, practical teacher. He demanded effort - not manual or mental labor, but the labor and sacrifice of the heart. In all this, though, there could be no ambition. That came from the mind. The labor we are talking of is a letting go and a service; it is to be more willing to receive; to accept a 'look from above'; to allow ourselves to be filled by the healing power of God's Love. This is the starting point for us all.

"All this our master spoke of in those first few days after he revealed himself to us. And then he set us to work.

"From what place, then, can an aspiring Christian begin? We can trust in God's grace but we have to participate, too. We have to be willing to submit to a deep examination of who and how we are. This submission, this surrender to being poor in spirit, is what the first beatitude points to.

"So we need to engage in a practice that takes us beyond mind's belief and conviction to a living experience of our true self. All action is sacred yet, until we come into relationship with the Divine, we will never find real meaning or lasting happiness.

"Time and time again our master returned to this theme of trusting in our own perfect wisdom. We began to see that, through meditation, we could find a place in ourselves that was beyond doubt, uninfluenced by thoughts and emotions. At first we could only get a glimpse of it yet it began to radiate its power in our lives.

"And so we began to use greater self-awareness to challenge ordinary mind and its sovereignty over our hearts. We learnt wisdom and compassion from these discoveries. What took us beyond the limitation of our selves opened us to receive the Grace of God and to more and more moments of being permeated by Love. We chose to struggle for a consciousness beyond emotions or the intellect. This is one of the root teachings of the Sermon on the Mount, given to the disciples by Jesus.

"To know God has to be a knowing that penetrates every

part of our body and being, our emotions and mind. So the only way we can serve the God beyond god (Our master used the term "praising the one true God") is to experience God within ourselves. To discover the true nature of this living organism is the first task of a Christian. This deep connection to our selves leads us directly to our rightful place in the healing womb of God's Infinite Light."

*"Words in a book, by themselves, mean
nothing unless you allow them to lead you
inside. All is already known within you.
That is where you must look."* *

---

* Hugh accepted a life of simple prayer. To him, that meant "remembering" God
for as many moments of the day as possible. One of the practices he used to help
him was to bring his mind to rest on a living inner idea or question.

He began to give me a taste of this. He would bring something in, which arrested
the flow of my thinking and led me to a deep contemplative pondering. I became
instantly more alive. It was as though what he said began to prise open a door to
God inside me.

I have included some of these sayings at the end of each commentary. This first
one came a couple of days after I arrived. I was in the library reading something.
The transcripts of the poor-in-spirit chapter were beside me on the arm of the sofa.
Hugh picked up the pages, ran his hands lovingly over the words of his master
and then, with a smile, placed them back down again.

CHAPTER V

They that Mourn

Two

Blessed are they that mourn: for they shall be comforted.

We are permeated by God's Love all the time yet we do not feel it. I am called and do not hear. His Love is a force that flows through every living thing and it finds its highest expression on earth when we know it in our selves. Only in this way can we ease the suffering of our Lord.

To mourn is a holy state of sorrow that God's Love is obscured in me. This is the beginning of the road towards Holy Desire; the beginning of longing for God, and the movement from my separate mind to the true feelings of the heart, which lead me to union.

I am far from home and alone. I mourn all that obstructs and diverts me from experiencing the love of God – that, too, is God's will. Lord give me the strength to suffer the mystery of your Will.

Let the fact that I do not devote all my attention to the presence of God in me be a source of deep sorrow. May I bear that struggle with resignation, patience and gratitude, and use it to feel God's Love, which is to praise the Lord.

God's Will is that my heart is closed to Him. God's grace is that my heart opens in suffering to him. Here, now, I am in the mystery of what it is to be human and, in that remorse, I find the obedience to serve. Only through mourning can I ask for the grace that will allow my heart to listen and to receive from the Vastness that which will make me free.

Jesus, the Nazarene, taught me this.
Lord Have Mercy.

Two: Commentary

"Wanting to live in God's love has to matter. It has to matter that we cannot feel that love in our hearts all the time. We have to care about that. There is a special suffering in our acceptance that there is in us what stops us from coming to God. We can call that special suffering "mourning".

"It is so easy to be satisfied with a life in which we only occasionally think about God. We must try to hold the presence of the Everlasting in all that we do every moment. However impossible to achieve that might seem, our conscious remembrance of the Divine is the only path that leads us away from the hell we create in ourselves.

"We have to care about our inability to be Christians – not in a way that creates shame or guilt but through a special kind of remorse for how things are as they are – this is mourning – a true Feeling beyond the ordinary emotions of regret or frustration, which are generated by the mind.

"To mourn is not an emotion. It is a deep ache in the heart of the soul that we do not feel God's look upon us all the time and cannot always hear the voice of God in everything we see and do.

(Ordinary emotions come from the mind and separate us from others. They are based on what we want or don't want at the level of the personality. They have to do with our sense of separateness and the unconscious fear behind our clinging to likes and dislikes. Even kindness can be offered in order to receive something back. Then it becomes - like fear and anger, desire and hatred - a manipulating response in pursuit of what "I" want and my service is lost to God.

As we progress towards a second emotional level, our tender sorrows, our joys, our open-heartedness and generosity of spirit rise within us as 'higher' emotions. These point us towards our common humanity and to the still wider realm of Feeling.

Feelings, themselves, come from the heart of our souls and unite us in God's mystery and are filled with grace and silence. Feelings are unifying emotions and belong to another level altogether. Christ, in one sense, reaches out to us through Feelings.

Feelings lead us to something larger than ourselves and point us higher, towards a relationship to Oneness and the vastness that is God. Shame, for instance, is a powerful emotion that traps us in the hell of the mind's own making and shrinks us away from openness. Mourning or "holy remorse" - the sorrow of being far from knowing God's presence - is a Feeling and, as a Feeling, it links us to a mightier world, holier than our own.

His master, Hugh said, described Feelings as "the true heart of our search for union". To experience a true Feeling is to feel the spirit of Christ in us).

"We can trust the Feeling of mourning. It cannot be thought or willed. To experience our separateness and mourn it from the heart is an authentic place from which to rest in our Christian practice.

"Another important aspect of mourning is that it's an antidote to the ambition of the mind. We saw it in ourselves so often. I remember, in particular, my jealousy when our master praised someone else. I wanted to be noticed and not be left behind and in that wish to be special there is a defiance of God's will. That is what creates hell in us. A direct challenge to that ambition is to accept that I am far from what I wish for and to remain *in the mystery* and the pain of that situation.

"The Feeling of mourning, then, is to begin to feel my separateness from God. It can be experienced in the pain of meaninglessness when the ego-mind has no answer to "who am I?" or to "why am I here?"

"Mourning links us to the higher world to which we belong - a world whose qualities are those of conscious love and which is only to be found in the present. All that we wish for exists in our connection to that world - a heaven whose flame exists in us, ready to be fanned by our practice.

"In all honesty, to try to move towards God as a Christian is the most treacherous of all journeys. It is so easy to lose our way. So often we discover when we turn to look that we have fed our ego-self and moved further away from where we most wanted to be."

Hugh paused for a while and I listened to the silence of deep night.

"Gently forcing the mind to relinquish its grip is the aim of all paths on the way to spiritual unfolding. The gradual dissolving of the self is achieved by opening the heart so that all in me can be bathed in the light of Holy Spirit, in Love.

"Our master was always reminding us that, however much our lives are governed by a mind that exiles us from God, we are never forgotten. The moment we see that we are far from our struggle towards the Divine is a moment given to us by His grace. The seeing of that is a moment of freedom. For just a few seconds we are not lost in forget-fulness and that moment has a feeling that is active, a feeling I can trace back to something alive in me. That could be called a moment of awakening to God's light.

"Once we choose to participate in the journey towards God, towards Love and our true home, we begin to feel the strength of the mind's defiance. The only thing we have as a defense against the ignorance of what it knows (and the delusions it tries to protect) is our heart and the Feelings that come in response to a call from above.

"Beneath the world we know, the world of form, there is a current of silence and stillness that offers us our true connection to the world. Our master stressed again and again that we had to find some sense of where we stood in relation to the Infinite and we had to feel that in our hearts. When our Christian search becomes more immediate and direct, everything our mind holds dear becomes less important.

"We can know this. When someone close to us dies, for instance, the truth of our own physical death is thrust upon us. For a few moments we touch the suffering that comes with the painful knowledge of all that will become lost to us. In the company of others, our hearts open, our perspective on life changes and priorities shift in their apparent importance.

"The soul's heart lives in Feeling in the simplicity of the present. There is no effort in embracing what is. Joy comes from living in submission to God without having to make the effort to constantly try to become somebody different. I am already here, complete and whole. I have never been anything else. Only when we are trapped in the mind is all that sense of wholeness and stillness obscured by stress and tension and anxiety. It is a world where all our desires for happiness separate us from God - the source of the one true lasting happiness we long for.

"In the meantime, separation is to be mourned. Contemplating our body's ending can also help that process, or at least how we hold *"in mind"* the inevitability of our own death and the death of all those around us; will we ever travel this way again? The present moment is already lost to us – where was I when it passed? These moments can become days and weeks, months and years in which we do not take part in the search for the All Mighty. Only when we participate in the struggle to open to God can we call ourselves true Christians."

Hugh was silent for a few moments. His voice took on a stricter tone when he began again:

"Even the placing of ourselves, as instructed in these first two beatitudes, is more than we can do. The attitudes they demand will only come as our practice develops but they can be the beginning of our aspiration to behave **as if** I could be a Christian. To move from emotion to Feeling has to be the result of inner work and faith – all of which are themselves, the Lord's gift. I am helpless before God. All I have is a feint wish that can turn my interest within and even that is given by God. All is God's. So where to begin?

"The only tool we have at our disposal to reach a direct experience of God is the body. By struggling to know a direct experience of our selves, we will find the Divine. We hold God captive in our bodies. All that obscures Divine Presence from our sight resides in our own bodies and has to be overcome and sacrificed to God at the hands of our compassion and loving kindness.

"Let the fact that we do not bring enough attention to the presence of God in us be a source of remorse and let us bear that sorrow with patience – even that can be used as part of our discipline and practice. God is always there; it is only me who comes and goes.

"We each are made by the same source; we each blossom in our own time; we are each in the other. It would be wrong to describe God's relationship with us as personal. That is a concept that belongs to our world, not His. His light shines on us all. Each of us is linked by Love and is merged in the vastness of God's love. In that sense, I can never be forgotten. The spark of God in us will always return, in the end, to the Light.

"To taste the presence of God and then to lose it again, as we must, is painful...especially as the refusal is always mine. If we accept that pain, then that is "to mourn". In that state of deep remorse and loss we can feel the promise of our return home – we are made whole and comforted. Re-establishing our link to the loving arms of the Infinite is the only healing we need."

"The Divine can always enter to change your situation. What would it mean here, now, to know that as something real in yourself?" *

---

* I can laugh at this now. There was a rickety old solid fuel stove in the kitchen with an oven door that was really difficult to close. I had been struggling with some recipe and slammed the door in frustration. I heard Hugh laughing. He had been watching me burn in my own anger and shared this.

CHAPTER VI

The Meek

Three
Blessed are the meek: for they shall inherit the earth.
The world is known by those who turn away from it. To bring my gaze back within myself is to experience all the forces of the universe and to know God in me. To be meek is to let go of all that I wish for myself and simply experience how I am in the immediacy of the present without judgement. Through a deep acceptance I allow my inner life to be lived in me by the Divine Will. If I try to change what is, I immediately lose the help of Holy Spirit. By imposing my own wish, I refuse free passage to God's Will. I am lost in a world of reaction where I serve a lesser God of my own invention who bends to my difficulties and whose will I obey only on my own terms - a false God who accepts duality.

How do I notice my state without the "violence" of a wish to change it? To look in the mirror of my life is to see what is, without imposing how I wish it to be: All that has happened, all that is happening and all that is still to happen comes from God.

In meekness I can experience the Divine Presence. Away from self-desire and self-aversion, in silence and stillness I can open to the mystery of God's Love – a mystery that exists in me and in everything.

So in meekness I allow God to take up my effort, to guide the gathering of my awareness so that I can receive Him in my body.

*I open to the heart of Christian practice – to accept that, without
God's grace, I cannot receive all that is my birthright. When the
Lord wills it, I turn my attention inside to find Him ever waiting.*
    Jesus, the Nazarene, taught me this.
    Lord Have Mercy.

Three: commentary
"To look for God is a look within. In this moment, things are
as they are; I am as I am. It is a sacrifice, a moment of
making sacred; to be alert and relaxed at the same time,
dissolving in me the tensions that refuse silence and the joy
of God's love.

"How do we allow God to lead our lives? To be meek is
to develop a Feeling for love and service to God. It is to
relax; to submit in trust, instead of seeking to conquer and
control our world on earth. It is the work of the heart to
refuse the will of the head.

"The more we struggle to win control of our lives, the
more speed and aggression we create to overcome our
obstacles and the more we become identified with 'worldly
cares'. These 'identifications' threaten the stillness through
which we can receive Holy Spirit and hear the Word of God.

"To be meek is to take in the impressions of my life
without the disturbance of reaction and judgement - just
noticing without placing a label of 'good' or 'bad' there. It is
a trust and a letting go. In practice, we have to develop
awareness of our inner life. We open the way to awakening
the spirit of Christ in us and to accepting the sacrifice we
must make.

"There must be no violence in this witnessing; no wish
for what I see to be different. It is a gentle opening to
something that is free of all that causes us to suffer in the life
created by our ego-minds.

"The heart of this message of meekness is that, through

acceptance, we become free of all we try to control and which, in turn, controls us. In that moment, we inherit a world that is true and walk upon Earth as it is and not as it has become distorted by how we wish it to be.

"Our master taught us that meekness is a cornerstone of all Christian practice. It allows us to be 'in the mystery of the coming and going of Holy Spirit' without clinging or intruding with our own opinions and beliefs, desires and aversions. Instead, we rest in a world created by God's will. I submit to His heart's desire, which becomes mine.

"Without this meekness, my self looks at the world and wants only what it likes. It imagines having all that it desires. It is only alive and expressive when it is wanting. That is its life's breath. The self seeks its happiness in perpetual wanting and so submits itself to an endless world of "never enough". The tensions and sufferings of not having are always there because nothing *can* be enough or the breathing would stop.

"And yet there has to be some kind of wish that leads me to Christian practice. To begin with, we bring our wish for things to change: our wish to be free. That, rather than our longing for God and the unbearableness of being apart from God, motivates our effort. We can mourn that and, at the same time, use it to bring us to the door of Holy Desire.

"God's Love pulses through all life and never stops its bidding to us to return. God is calling us all the time. Divine Love is there in us yet, without our awareness, its healing force is not available to us. We cannot serve consciousness in the way we should, if we do not feel the expression of this force in us. We go on transmitting only the scattered energy of our anger, fear and desires and the darkness we create obscures the Divine Light from our awareness.

"If, however, we notice; if we gather in the attention to witness what is taking place in our thoughts, emotions and bodies, we might be less angry, less afraid, and then, even in that small and incredibly miraculous way, God has had an action upon the world through us. Something, which appeared to have no possibility of transformation (we could call that 'hell'), was changed in us by God's Grace.

"All the exercises we were taught by our master had been given to him by Jesus. They were designed to harness this level of attention in order to allow what he called "the fourth holy attention" to arrive.

"Our master taught us that there are at least three different kinds of attention. The first is taken by any distraction or diversion; the second limits itself to a single problem or focus and we call this concentration. The third is an inclusive attention that offers us a greater awareness of all that is happening in the present – we can allow the noise and distraction to be there and still sit in silence in an attention that can be held by a self witness.

"There is also another kind of attention. This is a holy attention, which is independent of me. It carries God's grace and my task is to open myself to be able to receive it. It is an integrating force of wholeness that our master called Holy Spirit. It is a look from above and contains the Voice of God. It arrives in response to the spirit of Christ in me - the Holy Desire to return.

"Holy Spirit – God's emissary on earth, which brings with it the silence and true understanding of His Love - comes into our perception only when we are either in a state of deep stillness or when, in a place of despair, we let go completely and surrender our will to His. If we were wise, we would sacrifice everything for this.

"When Holy Spirit enters, we are open to another world of knowledge and understanding that is beyond the hierarchies of Man. It happens only in moments but its promise is always there and we must prepare ourselves in order to allow its coming.

"The force of our attention is the bridge between our 'sleep' and a state of spiritual awakening. We need to be in this state of awareness to receive the presence of silence through which Holy Spirit arrives. Our master said that we had a choice. We could turn our attention inwards or allow it to be scattered abroad. He said we had some control as to whether our attention was eaten up by the distractions of the external world or used to nourish a growing awareness of our inner life. It was he said, in effect, the choice between eating, or being eaten by, our own minds. Self-will can be used to turn the attention within. Later, something else takes over.

"Our master referred to all this as the Christian act of witnessing. The more we can take part in witnessing our own inner life and, in balancing it with a deep noticing of the outer, the more we are available to witness Infinite Oneness.

"To know what keeps us from God is useful. We can work on that. We can ask for God's Grace to help us. Our master would repeat, again and again, that there is always help.

"So in meekness, we can begin to receive impressions with a new kind of willingness. Every impression has the Divine Presence in it. We have to learn, first, how to look, then how to notice and finally how to see. These correspond to the three levels of attention. Only then, when we open to the fourth holy attention, can we say that I am looked upon, I am noticed; I am seen and remembered by God.

"The mind of the self will use 'trying to be a Christian' for its own self gain and revel in self-pride as it imagines its forthcoming enlightenment.

"The act of witnessing in the moment subdues the mind and its reactions and identifications and we can begin to experience everything arising in the present as being held in silence by the will of God. When the mind and the body are linked, in balance, the mind releases its grip and we are 'seen from Above'.

"Meekness, then, is emptiness of ambition. We must not allow the self in us to change our thoughts and emotions and sensations in order to be perfect. The body breathes and the mind thinks by itself and both can be seen as manifestations of the will of God. They are not for me to challenge directly. If we allow meekness as our response to all in us that refuses God, then it can be permeated by a healing light; then it is changed for us *not* by us.

"In witnessing where we are, here, now, in relation to the presence of God's love, there has to be less effort and more meekness. Resistance and agitation come in direct proportion to the strength of our self-desire for something. I push my wish forward and I clash, in open conflict, with all that I fear might stop it or might rob me of success. Already my desire for something brings with it the fear of losing it. If we search for God in this way, we will never find him.

"In reality, nothing can be owned. Divine Grace is the birthright of us all. Any results are not to be claimed by me. They belong to God. Even the emotions produced by the mind join a much larger, universal movement of energies. Our master tended to talk about energies more than emotions so that we would come to see that they passed through us as part of the cosmic order of things, rather like emotional weather fronts. If we allow them to belong to us, they feed our sense of separateness. Our master said we need to allow the forces of life to compose themselves in us...without allowing them to *be* us.

"We can begin to see these emotional energies in us through the transformative and integrative force of attention, of witnessing. We have to ask ourselves how we might respond with less attachment and more compassion, instead of being caught in reaction to them.

"If we do attach to our emotions, thoughts and desires, they become impossible to destroy. All we can then do is suppress them or deny them and, once that happens, we have lost the possibility of transformation. We cannot think our way past the mind. The more activated we become, the closer we move towards a fragmented inner world where we are lived by our thoughts, emotions and habits. This agitation opposes God.

"If, though, our attention is not taken and we can rest in the equilibrium of meekness, that thought or impulse becomes like a passing cloud in a larger sky and is robbed of its strength. We have, in that moment, been given, by God's grace, a taste of true freedom.

"In the harmony and balance that comes with meekness, we witness without attachment. To reach this state of freedom from emotions and thoughts takes a long and sustained effort and a precise guidance by a spiritual master. The grace of God that passes through Christ's teachings allows us to begin that journey by inviting the influence of silence and stillness into our lives.

"To breathe deeply and relax is to bring intelligence to the cells of our body. To be present to this process means allowing our attention to expand and become more inclusive.

"Our master taught us how to live with meekness in all aspects of our lives. It brought a wonderful grace and sacred attention to the way we acted and to all our relationships.

"Meekness allows us to let go of the tension of the mind and to move towards peace. We have to find the confidence to try that again and again – in effect, to hunger and thirst after righteousness.

"Relaxation is the theme of meekness. The sacred is stillness and silence, infused with the will of God.

"Christianity is the discovery of ourselves as the incarnations of the Divine. Purity of heart, emptiness of self, consciousness and opening to love, allow us to receive Holy Spirit. The One can then work through us in the resurrection of our service to the Everlasting; and Divine Love becomes a gift of new life, given to us by God in each moment we *praise* him."

"Everything you do and say has its source in the divine mystery. Everything is alive in this one ocean and behind it all is silence. That silence is always there in you." *

---

* The telephone in the house hadn't been working and I had used my mobile to make a call. I had put it down on one of the side tables in the living room and forgotten about it. Needless to say it rang loudly that evening and cut short Hugh in mid sentence. He sat there, smiling. I ended the call as quickly as I could and, still flustered, went back to my notes to try and remember what Hugh and I had been talking about. I heard him chuckling to himself.

CHAPTER VII

They which do Hunger and Thirst

Four

Blessed are they which do hunger and thirst after righteousness: for they shall be filled.

My longing to return must burn within me. In the gathering and dispersal of my attention I see the tide of God's purpose. I rise and fall, hungering and thirsting, upon this ocean of Divine Will, as I wait to be filled by Holy Spirit.

How close am I to the Divine? To know where God is in the life of my heart is my practice as a Christian, first and foremost, in every moment of my life. How open or closed am I to God's Love in the immediate present? Besides this constant enquiry, nothing else matters. This is the first step and the last step and the everlasting step towards God. I must learn to long for the Infinite and to transcend the mind that holds me back by submitting to the Holy pain of hungering and thirsting for all that God desires for me.

How do I find my way home? Raising my eyes to the Lord sets me free from the world of the mind, of flesh and matter. In my search for my own immediate Christian experience, I have to return to myself, again and again; to bring my awareness into my body to where I am; to change my state from forgetfulness to one of remembrance. I repeat this every moment by coming back to awareness. My aim is always to see how I am; the state of things in me...how far I am from God and how I can begin to open once more to infinite Oneness. My heart, like that of the Son, must break from longing to be with the Everlasting. I listen, always and forever, to the summons from Holy Spirit that reveals God in everything. I hunger and thirst for every moment, which offers me the gift of Christian renewal.

Jesus, the Nazarene, taught me this.

Lord Have Mercy.

Four: Commentary

"Christianity is beyond belief; it is the truth of experience. We can only receive God through the medium of our bodies. We have to gather our attention there so that we can feel Holy Presence within us and we have to hunger and thirst to return without getting caught in desire for a result. *We search, our master said, in order to participate, not to find.* We give ourselves up to that.

"We were taught that every moment is a call to be genuine. How do we respond to that challenge? We have to trust in our existence and our basic goodness. We are always being called. That call from above is always there. It is me that appears and disappears in forgetfulness of God.

"Our aim is to bring our awareness to how we are being lived by our thoughts, emotions and sensations in our bodies every moment. We have to set a sacred intention to struggle against distraction and so receive the energy of truth about ourselves – that we are divine. For that to happen, we need to see things exactly as they are; to bring the quietness of inclusive mindfulness and become more aware of the presence of God in my situation.

"By transforming the quality of our attention, we transform our consciousness and taste something higher in ourselves. Then we rest *in* Jesus in an alive vibrant energetic Christianity rather than trap our selves in a religion *about*

Jesus. It becomes an inner experience that continues to live in us, day in, day out, moment to moment, as we hunger and thirst for this understanding.

"This is the foundation that leads us towards Christian renewal. Resurrection is possible in every moment – that is God's merciful gift and our constant opportunity and hope.

"When our master talked about this, his eyes would light up with a fire that was impossible to describe. It was not excitement: it was a knowing that what we thought was impossible was, if we but knew it, inevitable. There was a certainty of joy in his eyes and we felt it, too, in ourselves over time.

"He narrowed everything down to this moment of "now" in a startling way: He said that we betray Christ in every moment when we do not struggle to remember God. This is the heart of where our betrayal lies. The link to the All Mighty - bringing God 'to mind' at all times – is so often broken and we are lost to Christ's urging and to the holy wisdom of the Spirit.

"Tension, anxiety and blockages of all kinds become the solid forms of our lack of remembering and the separation we feel from the Infinite Unity to which we belong. It is from this place in ourselves that we attend our churches and submit to our institutions and our higher authorities: we *need* to be told what to believe because we don't have access to the deep knowing in our own hearts.

"Our master told us it was so important not to believe but to experience; not to think but to feel the sacred in every thing. Instead, it has become safer for us to think our way into the future and to trust in the past rather than to rush, plunging into the aliveness of the ever-changing present moment. We are afraid. We know that it is here that our faith and our trust are truly tested. We hide in our craving for stability, form, certainty and security – the very things that are least permanent and which block our way to freedom and lasting joy.

"In silence our minds become afraid that what we already know deep within us will be heard; that some spark of our true intelligence in our hidden wish for meaning and the Love that unites all will demand that I turn away from my self and its commands.

"We are afraid of stillness because we fear it will lead us to a dark place where all that we fear in our selves will be set free. We will be alone there and we will remember that, at some point, our living bodies will die."

(Hugh said that mind fears the present. It demands the right to anticipate what is about to happen in the next moment. It needs the future to forestall the terror of the unknown by imagining how things will be. Our minds need time to create a future of their own making. All the effort, stress and tension in our lives are created by the fear that time - "my time" - will end.

With this constant threat upon it, our mind needs time beyond now to reinforce its sense of self in all kinds of material ways. In doing so, it produces so much distraction that we cannot free ourselves from the frenetic drama of life. We do not see the space that exists between thoughts or hear the silence behind all actions or feel the serenity behind every moment in life.

The terror in our situation is that the mind can possess a perception of Love and use it in its own service: then loving-kindness becomes grasping and needy, compassion pities, joy compares and envies the happiness of others and, in stillness, we become indifferent. We have to be willing to receive the Whole God; to reject nothing...anything less is to invite fanaticism. Only through a pure heart, can the Holy Presence from Above permeate the lower, which can then transform and evolve without violence – both in us and in the world...'Thy will be done on earth as it is in heaven').

"When we begin to look beyond the fears and dramas of

time, we 'raise our eyes to the Lord' in eternity. We create a far wider landscape from which to view life when we see it as an expression of eternity. From here, there is more stillness and we are able to contemplate God's purpose and will. It allows us to focus on the wonders of nature and to begin to feel our smallness. We are no longer so easily caught in the immediacy of life's anxious demands and the ego-mind's fear of their being no more time.

"Our master said that, as long as our attention is kept prisoner in the mind and in the will of the self, no amount of faith or hope can ever change us. We have to take hold of our attention and try, because the life of our souls depends on it.

"At first, all we have available to us as we begin our practice is sincerity and self-honesty. Wisdom, compassion, faith and love are *the results* of a struggle to experience ourselves and they grow according to our effort to attend to God's presence in us. The inner opening and closing to the voice of God is the real meaning of God's punishment and God's forgiveness and it points to the true meaning of sin.

"To draw back the energy of our attention from sensations and thoughts and from the emotions is a form a prayer. Then, if we could see, we would feel the movement towards God...but to feel that, our attention needs to be stronger than the distraction of our thoughts, emotions and physical movement.

"The posture, breathing and sensation exercises our master taught us were all linked to seeing what happens when we are in a state of prayer. Only in this state of silence and contemplation can we feel the illumination of God's Light upon us.

"As our holy desire grows in us, it meets the opposing strength-of-will of the self. The tension, which this creates, becomes the 'intentional suffering' and the only true war of the Christian warrior. This inner struggle, where we hunger and thirst, again and again, for the Divine in us, is the food and drink we lay before God in return for His Holy Understanding.

"Knowledge of our selves leads to faith; it is a knowledge that transforms us as we experience the action of the divine within us. Through this inner awareness we gain experience, which gives knowledge the opportunity to become wisdom and understanding: Understanding, which is the essence of Love, in turn strengthens faith.

"We have to ask: 'is this act or situation useful to me? Does it move me nearer to my aim?' If we apply our aim to love God, all action will be sacred and all situations useful.

"In this state of hunger and thirst, I am always in a place of being *in holy question*. Our master laughed when he told us 'it is not a question of having a question but of *being* the question'. It is painful to the mind to be forced to let go of certainty. It has lost its ground of safety as we enter a state of 'unattachment'…where only the heart can lead.

"To be *in holy question* in the midst of the Divine Mystery is a very profound state. The questions that terrify the mind – questions that don't have answers – are the questions that the heart likes best. Where are the Father, the Son and Holy Spirit within me? How does the Bible live in me? Where is my soul? Who am 'I'? What is prayer? In response, the self reveals its fear and tension while the heart begins to free itself from the prison of the mind's knowing.

"To let go of thoughts means to let them come and go; then it is our hearts that witness the immediate moment of our life. The heart has less investment in who we are and how we appear to others. It is less concerned with what exists than with what is arising. When we open to what is happening with compassion, the mind can let go of concepts and there is no need to think: there is just the movement of the universe happening inside and outside and we discover our natural being in righteousness.

"The intelligence of stillness and silence, felt in the heart, links us to the Divine Love that exists behind all life. Freed from their fear by the heart, our minds and bodies can serve the Vastness in which we become free and our hearts are filled."

"To be illuminated we need darkness. Within 'sin' there is always the sacred. To see the sacred in everything is to know Love's longing to be found in you." *

---

* Being with Hugh and Peter and listening each day to the depth of their teaching, led me, I'm afraid to admit, to a place where I felt special. One evening I began to impress Hugh with some deep insight I'd had. He must have caught my self-importance but he waited patiently for me to finish before speaking.

CHAPTER VIII

The Disciple

Hugh arrived one breakfast about halfway through my stay and said that Peter wanted to see me. Hugh, though, had something to tell me first. He sat me down in front of him at the table and launched straight in without any pre-amble.

"Our master, whose consciousness inhabited Peter, was full of love. God spoke through him. It was there for everyone to see. In obedience and surrender, our master had died to himself, as we all must, under the guidance of his own master, Jesus, 2,000 years before. If we look deeply within ourselves, we will see that our road must be the same."

"But your master isn't here now?"

"Our master left Peter's body last week when we were all in the Holy Land. His task was complete. That is why Peter is so depleted now. When our master returned once more to his rightful home, it produced in Peter a particular kind of exhaustion. His whole body, every cell, had been permeated by the intelligence of silence. Because he was so opened, he became extremely sensitive.

"Any kind of emotionally energetic disturbance was particularly disruptive to his system. All of these symptoms were foreseen by our master and he issued specific instructions for his care, once he had gone."

Hugh reiterated yet again that there was no need to believe any of what was being told to me.

I should, he said, trust my doubt and disbelief and approach the Gospel and what was still to be written with a critical, objective enquiry. The rest would take place by itself.

"There was also, for all of us in the group, a conviction that Truth has no earthly author. The nature of our master's embodiment of Peter and how that could have taken place, to us, wasn't important at all. It happened. The legacy of that – the holy understanding we experienced for ourselves – was all that mattered. We are clear that every word of this gospel has been written to help us escape from a place of betrayal in ourselves."

Later that morning, I went to Peter's room. He was sitting in a large armchair in pajamas and a dressing gown. His skin was not as white as it had been a few days before.

He fixed me with a searching stare. His pupils were almost completely dilated. Then his face broke into a grin and he asked me to sit in a chair opposite him so that he could see me more clearly in the shaft of daylight that broke through the gap between the curtains.

"I don't know how much Hugh has told you about our experience here but there are some things I want to say. If Hugh has already talked about them, let it serve to emphasize the importance of what I wish to share with you now."

He took a deep breath and seemed to gather strength to speak.

"We are dead to ourselves; we are dead to the presence of God. We have to become alive to ourselves in order to become alive to the Divine Trinity that can live again within us. Most of us do not hear God's Truth because we can no longer feel His Holy Presence in us.

"Through my master's instruction, we entered what he called 'Immediate Christianity' – a Christianity that offered a direct experience of God's Oneness. Our study and growing understanding of the beatitudes brought our practice alive. We experienced a re-birth in our search. We embraced again the spiritual role of the human body as the only point of contact between God and Man. We need the awakening of presence to help us.

"True spiritual practice produces love and real love brings humility to all aspects of our lives and, especially, to the day-to-day action of living together.

"He told us love permeates our cells. It brings with it consciousness, wisdom and harmony, alongside, peace, joy, kindness and compassion. It connects us to what is beyond our minds and bodies, which are, themselves, reflections of our capacity to receive love and to be remembered by God.

"There is no denying that, although his will and vision were turned away from earthly time towards eternity, he felt in his heart an urgency to encourage us to hunger and thirst after righteousness. I think he knew he couldn't stay in the world for a long time and his task was to somehow re-plant a seed that would take hold and grow for the benefit of the world.

"We were, he said, to begin a new journey that would take us deeply into a Christian practice within ourselves. We would then go out into the world again to measure ourselves against the forces that would try to lead us back into the realms of the mind. That movement out into the world began with our recent trip to the Holy Land and what took place there.

"My master held as his sacred responsibility, the removal of all those aspects of our selves that obscured the Truth – the reality of God. In that charge he was fiercely true to his aim. He worked tirelessly, with great compassion and loving kindness, to move us, little by little, towards understanding and the slow dissolution of the self's grip upon our will and minds.

"People need to bring all their attention to the task of becoming Christian and not be distracted by what happened to me...but perhaps I could say something. What is interesting is what is happening to me now, because it does reflect on the nature of our task as Christians.

"Let me say, first, that my consciousness was blended with the consciousness of a fully-enlightened disciple. To 'me', it was like a gradual transfusion of nectar and bliss that increased my health and vitality as it grew inside me. It freed me from my own fears and sufferings and, at the same time, it brought with it the smell of the desert and Judea two thousand years ago.

"The greatest of my suffering has nothing to do with my physical depletion and general weakness: It is that, when my master left me, he left someone who had not benefited from having to make any spiritual efforts of his own. I was alone and unprepared to face the embodied knowledge of my own nothingness: that I am not the 'me' that is called Peter, as you are not the 'me' that is called Robert.

"We are part of an indescribable Unity, the knowledge of which sweeps away all separation and identity. When our master's consciousness left me, I experienced the terrifying feeling of annihilation that can come with that realization. What was missing for me were the true, sacred and genuine feelings of faith, hope and love of the Divine that slowly grow alongside the gradual destruction of the self's belief in itself as separate.

"The others, here, had been able to develop that inner strength through the living, energetic presence of my master. I, on the other hand, had not had to rely upon the extended spiritual practice that usually produces these holy results in us and so I became absolutely defenseless when I was by myself again.

"It is difficult for me to explain what this meant but all that was available to me – all to which I had recourse to ensure my apparent survival - was total submission to the will of the Divine.

"Thanks to His Divine Grace, I entered the eternal darkness of God's humility. In that darkness, everything that was separate in me fell away and it was from there that God *knew himself* in me. I was raised above myself to a place where faith and hope have their true source. I was bathed in the certainty of God. All that remained in the emptiness was the unchangeable, immoveable Truth.

"Love is the energy, and His humility is the will, upon which the Universe is built. There was more to understand but it was not given to me to see and know what lay further beyond the darkness."

I could *feel* his visible joy and the bliss that glowed within him as he spoke.

"We have no need to fear. We *are* the Divine and its music is there inside us, whatever we do. Though we seem individual, we reflect the beauty of the whole. Why is it so hard for us to believe in a new beginning for ourselves?

"To live is to be aware in every moment. Life reveals itself in us through movement; through the gathering in and the radiating out of life in its silent form. Life ebbs and flows through the birth and death of every thought and breath and impulse, and through all else that begins and ends. Nothing in life, no thing, no moment, is ordinary. Love is the primary force of expressive life and the mind can only skim the surface of it."

Peter sat quietly for a long time before he spoke again.

"The beatitudes offer more than just a personal spiritual

practice. Man has a holy purpose on earth and the second four beatitudes deal with that purpose and the life that a Christian should lead in the world. It is a purpose far beyond what we could possibly imagine."

CHAPTER IX

The Merciful

Five

Blessed are the merciful: for they shall obtain mercy.

We are the darkness through which God's light shines. Love needs my darkness to illuminate the presence of God. I submit to being loved. In building an earthly home for Divine Presence to enter into me, I am offering Love my mercy and, in return, my life receives the true gifts of Holy Spirit – the mercy of Divine Love and Holy Wisdom.

The task of a Christian is to become a vessel for Love. I am filled with Holy Desire – not my own desire but the desire of God to express himself through me. My service is to open to Divine Will and, in doing so, I am opened to life.

As God is our beloved, so our souls are the beloved of God's Love. Through our souls' Holy Response, God knows himself.

I bring my heart to be filled with Christ's longing for the Everlasting. In that surrender, I offer my mercy. I am God's instrument when I live in humility and suffer His Will. All that I put before God is done in the name and spirit of Jesus Christ. In this way I rid my heart of the persecution of the self. I have to open myself to the influence of Holy Spirit as my guide in this. It floods its mercy, like water, into every place where love is obscured. Then my guilt and shame – the places in me that refuse to accept God's love - are transformed by new hope.

I feel God's mercy in the opening of my heart. To experience and accept this Law of Opening is to trust in the loving embrace of the Infinite.

Jesus, the Nazarene, taught me this.

Lord Have Mercy.

Five: Commentary

"All things come from Love and all things return to Love. Everything arises out of the vastness that is Love. Love is the affirming, creative force in all that lives in the universe. It is there, even within chaos and darkness.

"Love looks upon all things and that look is the very essence of all life. It enters all darkness in search of Holy response – the echo of God's Divine Love for itself. The obscuration of Divine Love is a matter of deep significance. Without witness in us, our own Holy response cannot return to serve God.

The Holy response of Man can only come from the heart of the soul. It lives in Christ's suffering. It recognizes life as a movement of eternal return.

"The profoundness of the Christian teaching is that God's Love permeates us and through Christian witness – through "Praise" - that Love is returned and ascends again in Holy response. That Holy response from man is the food that nourishes God in his kingdom. To offer back to God His Love filled with Holy response is the true and profound purpose of all Human Life on Earth...and the true meaning of "to be merciful".

"By gathering our attention, we energize the body to fulfill its true role: to receive God's love, here, now, immediately. From developing this inner human beingness, the life of the soul in eternity can come into existence and we can link the material world of the body with the formless world of the spirit. It is the heart of the soul that hears God and allows the action of Divine Light to pass through us into the world. This is our sacred task as Christians – to allow God's Love to have an action upon the world, through each one of us.

"Whatever we do – however forgetful we are of the Infinite - we cannot betray God. We have no choice but to serve. Turning, poor in spirit, towards God can happen here and now with our participation or we are left to begin our journey at some other time in the endless future of eternity.

"The higher God, the God beyond the Gods of duality and good and evil, uses us to speak to the world not in words but through love and silence and the intelligence of the heart. In choosing to open our hearts through our devotion, Love and silence can take hold, through us, on Earth. In struggling to be Christian, we lessen His suffering and ease His pain.

"What would it mean to rejoice in the Lord? What happens when we wish to live in the love of God but, instead, are filled with hate, anger and fear? How do we respond to our humanity? We have to be merciful and bring compassion to ourselves, first, before we can offer it to others – not passively but with the remorse of our 'sin' in our hearts.

"True repentance only comes through the touch of Holy Spirit and we feel the sorrow of our Lord when we witness our own forgetfulness of God: then we see our 'sin'."

(According to Hugh, their master never used the word "sin" in an accusatory way. We sin without fault because we have no means to control our actions in our forgetful state. We are lost to God. All we have to set against this helplessness is a desire to be touched again by Holy Spirit so that we can be reminded that God lives and moves in everything).

"The idea of sin and virtue belongs to our world of

duality and not to the Divine Unity. Do I really see sin in others? What is happening to me when that takes place? Is not God at work in them, too?

"Our sin is not our personal possession, neither is our virtue. The nature of sin is to find ourselves so far from God and to remain deaf to his call, bidding us return. How do we allow God's mercy and forgiveness to live in us...not just in response to the suffering we see around us but to my own, which is the same? To allow myself to face suffering in this way is the real meaning of communion.

"As Christians we belong in this world, yet we bear the knowledge of a mightier one that lives in us. To see the patterns of a life governed by mind and to learn, instead, how to use our hearts to celebrate God in all things is how we offer our mercy to both worlds.

"We offer the Infinite our mercy when we are merciful to our selves and rejoice in all that we see. To bring judgement is to cease to rejoice. Mercy is to be free of judgement, to be open.

"If God's mercy is freely given, who are we to deny mercy to our selves and to our neighbors when we witness the presence of our refusal of the divine in our anger, fear and desire?

"So much of that refusal belongs to those aspects of our selves that learnt long ago to survive without love, and now, as we draw closer, we fear love will destroy us. The great sickness of our world is that we are afraid of love – the very thing we long for - above all else.

"We fear that somehow our material life will disintegrate around us, if we commit ourselves fully to Christian practice. All my possessions and relationships will become worthless to me and I will wish to retire from the world alone and naked of all I have known and loved. I will no longer recognize myself.

"This is how the self imagines things will be, if we take up the task of surrendering to God's will. Its fear guides it. It is not like this for most of us. The holy process of opening to the spirit is one that happens slowly. Our will cannot determine the speed with which this opening occurs in us: that belongs to a greater design.

"True, there is a surrender that needs to take place; a daily dying that involves looking towards God inwardly. We must notice when we look towards the external with our desires and how this severs the divine link. We have to abide in the word of God – in stillness and constant witnessing.

"From this place of witnessing we can know when we are alive in God and when we are dead to Him. We are touched by Holy Spirit when our attachment dies to the ordinary world and we raise our eyes to heaven. We see and are seen. In the same way, if we open to love, we will be opened to the Love of the Lord that is in us already. Then there will be no inside or outside; no "me" to get in the way. It is the love that can only be known by my soul's own heart.

"The birth of our new life as part of the Divine Unity happens gently and lovingly...and how could it be different? What we are asked to do is *allow* ourselves to be loved by God. We are not even asked to give up anything. That will be done for us, in meekness and in mercy, when *I am loved.*

"So we are not destroyed: we discover our perfection. The struggle is to allow that process to happen. To become a living sacrifice to Divine Love is to become merciful and to obtain mercy."

Hugh paused and looked at me to see if I grasped what he was saying.

"The force of Love, which has as its essence understanding and silence, is incredibly powerful. Love, even with its lightest touch upon us, influences the world. When we are quiet and merciful, for instance, we are not adding to the world's fear and anger...that is its own miracle.

"Through our Holy response we allow God's word to sound within us and we know his mercy. The Lord's Love grants us the grace of silence and attention and we are set free from our fears and the anxiety of nature – the hell in which we live. Then, we are led by the power of Jesus Christ and the merciful compassion of Holy Spirit to the Kingdom of God."

"When you feel stillness in your body, you are feeling mercy. At that very moment your body belongs to something greater than your self. So often the miracle of this passes us by." *

---

* I had been for a long walk one afternoon through the rolling, wooded countryside that surrounded the farmhouse. Released from my laptop and the business of writing, my body had revelled in the fresh air and in the freedom of movement in open space. Later, over tea, Hugh had recognised the change to my inner state.

CHAPTER X

The Pure in Heart

Six

Blessed are the pure in heart: for they shall see God.

The only heart's desire God allows is the longing to be with Him. Even that, at the end, has to be renounced. Then I can be born anew in the light of the Lord's Divine Love. Accepting my death, I become, at last, alive.

God can only be known by a heart that is empty of the needs of the self. It is a heart that has given up its wish to be free and happy. It loves for Love's sake and, through it, my soul returns in devotion to its source.

Divine Love leads me to be tested on the Cross of two worlds - this world and the next. To be aware of the touch of Divine Love is to be burnt by the Lord's command that the self cannot pass into the kingdom of God. In that moment, I am reminded and re-directed to the resurrection of our true purpose on earth. God's terrible resolve is to rid me of my self. Only then am I pure in heart.

I must abandon the arrogance of searching only for a connection to Heaven. I also belong to this world and the acceptance of both - of the whole of God's Will - is the essence of what it means to enter the place of pure in heart. Only this heart can witness and live Holy Truth.

The bridge between heaven and earth is Love. I have to let the divine illumination from above enter me. I allow myself to be led by the spirit of Christ, which, in the midst of my suffering, reveals the Oneness behind all life and bids me sacrifice all that my self wishes to the bliss of everlasting Love. Through Jesus my heart opens to Holy Spirit and can once again hear the true voice of God...the voice of One that exists motionless behind all movement.

Jesus, the Nazarene, taught me this.
Lord Have Mercy.

Six: Commentary

"Only through a pure heart is God's prayer heard in the world.

"To pray from a pure heart is to link the wish of my soul to the will of God. When we are wholly with God, there is no need for prayer. The Lord creates in us the desire to pray because he sees in our separation what we need. In that moment, He has already granted all that He persuades us to pray for.

"Prayer is not a demand but a response to God when we know the touch of Divine Love. Then we receive Holy Spirit and are lived in silence and understanding. We are One. We have died to ourselves in the most blissful way imaginable. We are God's love. We are filled with his Presence. In this state, we are in prayer. We cast a light upon the world from the burning away of our own self. 'Thy will be done' is all there is to pray for.

"Through silence, we have to be willing to die to our selves a little every day, and to all the desires and distractions that govern the self. Nothing else will do, if we wish to find life in God. To accept God's will is the prayer of all things living.

"At its most profound, our master said that 'all life prays'.

"The door to God is always open and we must strive, always, to place our selves in sacred submission to His will.

With our faith in the love that lived in him, we enter the same place of suffering as Christ – in stillness and silence we witness God's creation and bear the pain of knowing that we are not yet one with the Infinite. This becomes our place of crucifixion.

"The truth that Jesus gave us in his living example is that we can be filled with Holy Spirit and, through it, live in a new way on Earth. We cannot ignore Earth in pursuit of heaven alone. We have to acknowledge that we belong to two worlds simultaneously – the flesh and the spirit. All we can do is allow both to meet in us and wait to receive the grace of transformation.

"To be pure in heart is to stand before all life in flawless acceptance of my cross. Instead of a slave to the external, we can be slaves to that which would set us free. Then, all we see in the world outside points to God's presence and our darkness is permeated by the Divine Light.

"To be open to the will of the Everlasting is to be in that place of receiving, beyond what we can know: we are alert, active, present to witnessing, without the safety of certainty. Here, in stillness and silence, the heart allows us space and time to feel and understand more. We are open to another current of life completely.

"We feel a call from God, a new energy that carries in it my true potential as a human being. When it comes, we receive spiritual intelligence that hints at God's will and we experience a knowing that belongs to the heart, not the mind. Then there is nothing to do but live from a very particular kind of openness, which our master called a state of 'holy question'.

"This does not mean to have a question in front of us because then we are already searching for an answer. To be in holy question is to risk being open to the full impact of all inner and outer revelation. It is a state of constant alertness to 'presence'; to receive God's look from above upon us, free of self.

"By opening our Feelings and our hearts to their fullest extent, we allow life to express itself through us in communion with all other human beings. From here, we contribute to the evolution of the world, creating harmony, balance and silence in all our relationships and offering back to God His Love filled with our Holy response.

"All that happens, all that exists, points to immeasurable, Infinite Oneness. To be in holy question removes all that obscures us from seeing God in every aspect of the lives we experience. To be in holy question is to sacrifice everything of the self and to live life in deep trust of God's Will."

(God's Will cannot be known by the mind. It exists in the movement towards love, wholeness and holy return and can only be felt from a place of pure-in-heart. His Will is to be known as the holy intelligence that comes with the arrival in us of Holy Spirit. When we know God's Will, we are guided by His Love in all we do.)

"Inner openness to Truth is the sacred task of the pure in heart. The world of duality and opposites and the kingdom of heaven can meet in us and come into balance. The lower exists to allow the higher to express itself properly in the world. By allowing ourselves to be permeated by the higher, we are, ourselves, transformed.

"We let go of a desperate desire to know the future. The past is gone; the future is not yet here. All we have available, all that is truly accessible is our experience of the sacredness of life in this present moment. It is the only place where we can live deeply in the Divine Light that illuminates all things, and the only organ capable of it is the heart. If we can do this, then we have allowed God to take hold of our lives.

"A pure heart gives us the courage to live our lives,

offering grace and kindness to ourselves and to others. A pure heart is merciful. We experience the suffering of others as our own. A pure heart is compassionate. A pure heart is forgiving because to forgive allows us to love. A pure heart offers love, compassion, joy and freedom from the unconscious suffering we create.

"Our master was pure in heart. He could not bear to be apart from the constant presence of God's endless Love. For us we can only live AS IF this was possible. To live "as if" is to set an intention, a wish that Love be there: it avoids the self trying to make the feeling happen.

"He said that, even though it could take many lifetimes to become "pure in heart" we could still live 'as if' this were true for us now. It is important that we work *as if* we were Christians. We have to embrace love from the level at which we can receive it. Then we can begin to serve.

"Trying to live *as if* we knew God's grace, led us to it. We lived as though God was there and he came! We were pretending what was already true and so it became our truth. It was very much part of what led to our spiritual rebirth within the community.

"Only the pure in heart can see God so we have to act *as if* our hearts were pure - as if we were Christians -- while building the real Christian inside us. The bridge between our soul and the kingdom of God, to which it belongs, is attention, the medium of transmission that allows the permeation of our ordinary nature by Holy Spirit to be known by us. It is the sensation of presence. I AM. Through the link of attention, the body will willingly submit to the heart, which, in turn, allows Christianity to unfold within us.

"All that exists in the world - every energy - composes itself within us. We are lived by what is beyond our under-standing. God's divine message is written in our bodies.

The pure in heart are willing to bear the truth of that under-standing...and with its coming, the heart accepts in joy the sacrifice of self as the cost of receiving God's Love. The joy and beauty of Love lies in the depth of our heart's willing sacrifice."

"*Nothing can happen inside you in secret. No thought or emotion is unseen. Your choice is to become part of that seeing, now, in this moment. Be present to it. Grace lies behind everything that happens.*" *

---

* This came about just before we began work one day. Peter's recovery had been progressing steadily and Hugh and I had been able to start meeting in the afternoon and evening, rather than late at night. I had arrived caught up in some negativity and heaviness of my own. Hugh asked me how I was feeling and I tried to fob him off with "I'm fine". This was his response.

CHAPTER XI

The Peacemakers

Seven

Blessed are the peacemakers: for they shall be called the children of God.

To spread Silence is to spread the Word of God. To be in silence is to be touched by Holy Spirit. Without silence I cannot hear God in me nor see God in the simplicity and balance of nature and in all her wonders. In silence I am understood. In silence I am seen. In silence Love knows itself through me.

Silence brings unity. When I belong to silence, I am no longer alone but part of the vastness of the Divine. Turning towards the direction of my source and resting in that stillness, I become again, for a moment, a child of God. My life and all that I am arises out of that silence, in the presence of God, as does everything existing.

All life is engaged in one spiritual journey of birth and death. By allowing life's flow to express itself through me, I see God's essence in all action. Through this innocence, I participate in the silent movement behind all life.

The peacemaker is born in silence from a birthplace in Love. Listening in that silence, I free the world from my self.

Jesus, the Nazarene, taught me this.

Lord Have Mercy.

Seven: Commentary

"Silence frees me from identification, from worldly cares. Silence is the word of God. It is a state when we no longer fear life. In the silence I am no longer separate and fragmented and the creative word of God is heard. In this state, the love of God can spread through the whole of me. It spreads wherever it can, like a smile. It opens hearts and reminds us of what we are supposed to be. We are loved through.

"Our master began to instruct us early on in a daily practice and referred again and again to what it would mean to live as children of God.

"First and foremost, he taught us to act more mindfully and to bring qualities of grace and simplicity to everything we did. We began to live without so much self-consciousness.

"Gentleness, precision, care, attention – these were all words that we brought to mind whenever we chose to do something. Everything we did, in fact, became a sacrifice in the true sense of the word – to make sacred.

"We began to experience the peace of dignity and calm. To begin with, we applied Christianity, most specifically, to our bodies. We learned that the body is truly the temple of the living God and that it flourished through the meekness of moderation rather than through the 'violence' of over-indulgence. We exercised to remove tensions and to notice where in us we experienced antagonism. Fitness, health and an active relaxation all became sources of energy and help in our inner practice.

"Outwardly, our environment began to reflect the changes that were happening inside us. The appearance of the farmhouse, gardens and outbuildings were transformed.

"As we developed peace-making in us, we became more

conscious of beauty and harmony. Flowers and plant arrangements began appearing in the house with a lot more regularity. Clutter disappeared. We cleared surfaces and placed objects within space that honored their impact upon us. Furniture was repaired and cared for. What we didn't need was given away. We began to take in fresh impressions in a more attentive and receptive way. We felt the receptivity and responsiveness of the feminine unfold in us and realized that God is beyond the limitation of father or mother.

"We began to have a sense of what was enough and that spread into other aspects of our lives – what we said, how we moved, the amount of energy we expended on various jobs around the house, as well as eating, walking and dressing.

"The idea of cleanliness being next to Godliness took on a new meaning for us. Every moment could be more lucid in the sense that it offered us a clarity and spaciousness that encouraged our aim to live more fully in the present. This kind of 'cleanliness' came to mean mindfulness instead of mindlessness.

"Our attitude to food, cooking, cleaning up, clothes, our rooms and the whole of our environment became more graceful. We developed a relaxed discipline that began to harmonize our actions with the external world. This discipline did not feel imposed but gently informed and energized our contemplative practice. It allowed a relaxation that opened us to silence.

"We came to experience how all our actions reflected our own inner attitudes to the world and ourselves, from moment to moment, whether it was connectedness and kindness or isolation and resentment.

"We came to live 'as if' we were permeated by God's love rather than separated, lost and deaf to his call.

Through the 'making' of peace within ourselves, we slowly attracted in us an openness and an inner attentiveness. We noticed we were less affected by the confusion and anxiety of the world; by its excitements or depressions. Instead, we felt more delight and energy and freshness. There was something almost childlike in its purity and innocence that expressed itself through all we did. We became again wholly-participating Children of God, full of delighted curiosity and wonder at the inner and outer worlds in which we lived.

"How do we bring grace and harmony into all aspects of our lives? How do we approach all we have to do today with God's grace? This movement towards gracefulness and beauty, through our speech, thought and actions, allows us to embrace the presence of the Divine more fully.

"We give grace to our bodies in what we eat and how we speak and how we act. We give grace to our minds in how we hold the Lord in mind and maintain our attention towards the Infinite. We give grace to our hearts when we open to loving kindness, joy, and peacefulness. We give grace to our souls when we trust in the Trinity to guide us through our day.

"Everything that we did and witnessed brought us inwards to our Christian practice. Our eyes became turned towards God in all we saw and did. We learned to respect our relationships and listen to all other points of view: each life carries a sacred message that instructs us, if we listen. Everyone is our teacher and we are all pupils.

"Through this, we acknowledge that God exists in all things and that we can prepare for God's presence to be felt in us by the way in which we live our lives. We can bring a natural order to even the most mundane aspects of our day. Nothing can be separated from the Divine Unity of life.

"When we act in this way with our attention on God, His

Divine Light suffuses our ordinary lives. The mind can dwell either in light or darkness, yet it refuses the Light of the Lord's Love, which can move us from imprisonment to freedom and dissolve the dark that obscures the Divine in us.

"More and more often, we have to turn our captured attention away from the external world to witness God's presence in all that we see and do. That act brings peace and light and inclusiveness to our world...the blessedness and innocence of the peacemaker. From there, we can offer back our attention and love to the chaos and violence of the external world, which is, itself, only a reflection of all we hold within us. The inner and the outer meet, as one, through the peacemaker.

"The level of this inclusiveness and mindfulness extended to all elements of our ordinary life right down to the tea we drank. Did we celebrate its journey to us – the sun and the rain that grew it, the lives of the people who worked on the plantation and picked it? How did we add the boiling water? How did we raise the cup to our mouths? Did we pay attention to the taste on our tongues; to the passage of the tea through our bodies; to the way we placed the cup down again on the table or in the saucer? This became our silent praise of God from the center of our bodies.

"At dinner we had to serve each other and wait, without asking, to be served by someone else. Each had to be aware of the needs of others and trust that their own needs would be noticed and met. The way we lived began to manifest kindness and goodwill. Our movement became more elegant and graceful. And we began to acknowledge beauty in a new way, not just as a gift from God but as a link to the contemplation of wholeness and unity.

"As we led this more graceful life full of simplicity,

harmony and a natural goodness, we became happier. Our lives took on a natural order and, for some strange reason, there was a lot more time.

"Our lives became more silent but it was a living silence that pointed beyond itself; not the passive silence of ordinary relaxation.

"Contraction and tightness and tension became far more obvious to us in that new, more harmonious way of living our lives and were replaced by a stillness and serenity that helped our aim to love God. From here, we discovered that all action is sacred and all situations are alive and useful to us.

"Peace of mind is good for us and for others. To relax around our worldly cares and to address them here, now, in the present, is a way of taking care of our future.

"We learned to make ourselves more welcoming and accessible to others – both in our home, in our behavior and in our relationships. Making our space sacred evokes wisdom, intelligence, and balance – openness...and we bring that to the world in which we must live.

"Everything has to be brought into awareness. We need to feel the oneness of the body - our inner unity and inner integration with the outer, the greater unity. From here we can harmonize and connect to the outside world. This practice produces an equanimity in us that allows our attention to free itself from the influence of our thoughts and emotions and external distractions. All the impressions we receive through this alert attention become fresh and new, immediate and vivid.

"There is no doubt in me that the arrogance of trying to impose a mental control over our lives creates aggression and destroys our natural and intuitive openness and leaves us to enter the world from a contracted, defended place in ourselves. Instead, we can spread grace through a relaxed, sensed body. We develop a sacred mindfulness and attention in all the relationships we have to our possessions, our families, our friends, our environment and ourselves. It even affects our posture and how we stand and move, how we hold ourselves in our lives before God.

"From here, I am the breath which rises and the breath which falls. I am in balance, at peace, a child of God. In this way we move out to others through our gentleness and energized participation and spread Christianity, in its true sense, before us."

"What do I serve?" *

---

* Away from our writing, Hugh and I followed a strict daily routine. We rose early every morning to watch the sun rise, whether it was visible or not, and then sat in silence in the meditation room for an hour. We did the same at sunset. There were also other shorter meditations before lunch and before bed.

One lunchtime, towards the end of my stay, Peter joined us. His unexpected presence had an immediate effect upon the atmosphere in the room and I dropped into a deep stillness. At the end of the meditation I sat there, not sure what to do. I was just about to get up when Peter said this. The words still reverberate through me when I think of them now.

CHAPTER XII

They which are Persecuted

Eight

Blessed are they which are persecuted for righteousness' sake: for theirs is the kingdom of heaven.

I cannot see God in others until I see Him in myself. I cannot see love and forgiveness in others until I know them in myself. Through the darkness in others I see my self more clearly. I am persecuted by all that takes me away from God yet only through that persecution can I feel the strength of my wish to return and the power of Christ's spirit in me. And so I measure myself constantly against the strength of what would obscure the Divine Presence in me.

If I move away from the suffering of others for fear of it destroying my own happiness, I place myself in loneliness and separation. To be persecuted is to suffer the distractions of the outside world that break the silence through which I hear the call in me of Christ's wish to return. Though I live on the cross of two worlds, there is no choice but to return to God.

All that resists the Love of God is in me. If I turn to allow myself to be persecuted by that, I meet in myself the suffering that has belonged to Man since time began on earth. Only then can I feel love's movement in me. If I persecute others, I persecute God. I submit, instead, to living the passion of Christ within me.

The justice of the Lord is not the same as the justice of man. In

heaven there is only oneness: There is no punishment and reward,
no good or bad, no virtue or sin. There is a call in the silence to
Love and I must obey.

Jesus, the Nazarene, taught me this.
Lord Have Mercy.

Eight: Commentary

"All desires for happiness have behind them the one desire
to return to the bliss of God's Love. All that exists seeks in
its own way, to return.

"We have to accept that what persecutes us is sacred. The
sacred exists in everything. Everyone's actions are sacred –
known by God and motivated by His Will. This is the holy
understanding to be gleaned from all behavior we witness
in the world. Everything has God in it. If I am persecuted, it
is God who persecutes. If I persecute, I am persecuting God.

"At the ordinary level of our lives, we are persecuted by
our own desiring minds and by the desiring minds of
others. My wish to bring my attention inside in search of
God is denied again and again by the siren distractions of a
material world of form in which we all feel alone and
incomplete and seek pleasure as consolation.

"We are persecuted from within. We witness in others all
that we do not wish to accept about ourselves, including our
own inner betrayal of Christ. The darkness of shame and
judgement that then attacks us, as a persecution from an
unloving world, only resonates with what we already feel
there, within us.

"All this becomes important when we look at how we
project our reality on to the world. If I am fragmented and
angry, I see a world that is fragmented and angry. If I am
whole, I see wholeness. If I love God, I see the Love of God
in everything. All that I accuse in others is only what I am
blind to in myself.

"If I hate and kill those who oppose my God and religion, it is simply externalizing the hatred and murderousness I feel towards some darkened inner part of myself that contradicts what the mind insists on believing.

"Jesus taught his disciples how to meet their own darkness and their own inner persecution. He offered them Love as the way…a Love that can only exist in the present."

(Hugh spent a lot of time talking about the importance of Jesus Christ in our lives as a 'living mentor' that leads us through our suffering. The symbol of Christ's passion was a 'holy feeling' within us of blissful sinking into pain and suffering in the name of the Divine Love that unites. He didn't mean, by this, ordinary pain and suffering but the deep pain of mourning all the separation from God's Love that exists in the world.

He saw Jesus as the inner experience of an intense impulse of longing through which we can be given the will to die to the world of the small self and accept new life in God's light. We have to feel this Holy Desire of Jesus in us when we suffer by being crucified, in effect, between all that wishes for, and all that denies, my openness to Holy Spirit. Through this, we can, he said, feel deeply into Christ's suffering, know it as our own and be willing to allow it to transform our lives).

"This 'sinking into suffering', our master said, is about being willing to bear whatever emotion is in us and know it for what it is. If we can stay with what is painful and unpleasant and seek to understand that it is no different to pleasure, we are being persecuted for righteousness' sake and the kingdom of heaven is felt in us. This is conscious suffering and it produces very precious results.

"Jesus Christ can become our inspiration. He reveals to us how he embodied God's love even though he too, like us, was caught in the suffering of belonging to two worlds – the vertical world of spirit and the horizontal world of earthly flesh.

"The horizontal and the vertical together form the true meaning of the Cross and, with an open heart, I have to plunge into the persecution of this. God chooses that this be so. This has to be pondered and properly understood.

"We betray Jesus in ourselves every moment when we do not hear the Word of God in what we do. We are not listening. We are identified with the material world. The horizontal plane of life attracts our attention away from the vertical plane of spirit. Prayer becomes our willingness to suffer in order to return to the Infinite, as our Lord Jesus Christ did. *We become a living crucifixion.*

"A compassionate response to the *unconscious* suffering of others is also part of what it is to be a Christian; to have the courage to be vulnerable and to receive the impact of the pain of another, which can come as anger, fear, despair or hopelessness and depression. In return, I cease to become separate from mankind and experience a deep sense of connection. How does this happen? I enter the realm of the heart. This is so important because the natural impulse of attention is to open, just like the heart.

"In truth, we are all full of agitated thoughts and emotions and this fragmented energy from within ourselves spreads out to persecute others. How do we meet it as a Christian in a new way? How can we embrace the truth of suffering?

"I can love my neighbor because I can see him *as myself.* To love thy neighbor is not to be reduced to external kindness or help; it is a deep touching of the soul that their pain is experienced as the knowing of our own pain; that we are the same. In that moment, we grant God His greatest wish.

"Not to be able to love my enemy is to remain bound by a lesser love that is earthly. Divine Love – the love that burned in our Lord Christ - includes all. Only by knowing persecution do we come to feel in ourselves the strength of the wish to be made whole, in the spirit of Jesus.

"If there is struggle, then it is in this; to reclaim the peace, compassion, love and joy that is our rightful inheritance, through our return to connection and relationship in the Love of Christ.

"God's love is always there like a mighty river calling to us from afar on its way to the ocean of Divine Oneness. That river is within us but only when its roar is heard does it take us with it. Once we enter there is no return. Our persecution is to see how our ignorance keeps us stranded on the riverbank, clinging to safety...and how our sense of oneness escapes us, again and again.

"Can we see that we all arise from the same field of stillness; that the space between the nucleus and the wall of my cells is the same as in all other living things *and in that space are all the forces of the universe - especially Love*? We are the same thing, though seen in the myriad variety that is nature's expression of all life.

"How do we receive all that wishes to be known and felt through us? How do we remain silent enough to be fully open and receptive to God? The only way is by being in the present and living within our bodies, free from the concept of death, the fear of which governs our actions and feeds all the conflict and violence that exists in the world.

"Our master taught us to trust in the well-being of the world. God's Love shows itself in all aspects of our lives and permeates all actions of the world. If, through our minds, we doubt our goodness, we become closed to the qualities of loving kindness, joy, compassion and peacefulness...and we lose our trust in the completeness of others.

"We must see and feel how others suffer as we do; how they, too, permeated as they are by the Love of God, cannot hear the call to return that is always there.

"All of this demands our opening. We have to open our hearts, if we are to further the welfare and evolution of Mankind. We have to allow our hearts to be seen as completely as we can. Beneath the anxiety and stress, the speed and the aggression, despair and the violence, there is the creative force of Divine Love without end. The tragedy of our lives is that we cannot see that right here, now, nothing is missing. We are complete.

"This beatitude tells us to know persecution as God's will; to suffer it with resignation, patience and gratitude and to meet all that is in the world with warmth and interest, appreciation and delight.

"In the vastness of eternal unity, real Love brings holy understanding and links us to all others through our shared suffering. Despite the blindness that forces us to swim unconsciously against the tide of Divine Love, that wondrous, holy power on Earth links us all and moves us – despite all we do - unceasingly towards the Everlasting. Ours is the kingdom of heaven. There is no escape from God's Love."

"I belong to Heaven and to earth. To become Christian - to obey love as the most important thing in my life – would allow these two worlds to meet in me." *

---

* This came up after one of my trips to the local supermarket. To move from the silence of the farm to the noise and sensory assault of large numbers of people going about their shopping was a shock. I lost all hold on my inner attention and found myself recoiling from the experience. Once more, the energetic change in my state was immediately obvious to Hugh when I arrived back.

CHAPTER XIII

HOLY FELLOWSHIP

The willingness to reach for God holds in it the greatness of all human enterprise. We are bound together in the holy fellowship of human suffering – the suffering of separation.

The gentle unfolding within us of Divine Light restores the quality of our hearts to their true nature in tenderness, openness, softness and warmth. Yet the link to the Divine cannot be sustained without silence, and grace cannot be felt without our surrender to stillness. So our first task is to allow silence and stillness to enter us. When we do this, we are engaged in a living experience of Christianity.

Several times during Hugh's explanation of the Gospel, he mentioned inner "exercises" that had become part of the group's spiritual practice but, as the end of my first visit to the farm approached, he had still said nothing more about them. I mention this because, as I began preparing to re-enter the world again, I felt a real need for something I could practice by myself; something that would support me and allow me to ground the teaching in my own daily life.

I raised the question with Hugh and he spent a long time that day with Peter. It wasn't until the next afternoon that he sought me out to share what had been decided.

"I asked Peter what you should do. He said: 'receive the divine". Then we sat in silence for a long time."

Hugh laughed.

"More often than not, you can learn far more from a few words than from a lot. In this case, Peter trusted those three words would lead me to the answer."

"Did they?"

"Yes."

I waited in silence until he spoke again.

"You remember I referred to meekness as *the cornerstone of Christian practice*? The meekness I am talking about does not have the modern connotation of passive compliance. To be meek, in the terms our master referred to, is to have the courage and the faith to allow the active quality of gentleness to enter all aspects of our lives. It is a vital, powerful force in its own right, able to transform the way we live. It points us towards holiness and to the sacred stillness behind all movement. From that place in us, all the beatitudes can unfold.

"So my proposal is to invite you to 'practice gentleness'. When you understand what gentleness is, you will see that its simple presence can have an immediate effect upon our lives and it is available to us right now. Gentleness is within our reach in this present moment, just as we are and it, quite literally, brings us alive."

"What is it, then?"

"That is for you to discover. We can begin to experience it as a wholehearted, clear-eyed, confident trust. Through gentleness, I can dare to live in a way that feels much more connected. I am able to really look upon this world of ours and risk opening fully to it, in true Christian fellowship with all life...not in a nervous, sideways glance or with my head bowed but by feeling the full-in-the-chest impact of the wonder of life on earth, its vibrancy, its color and all its mystery.

"So gentleness demands courage. It inevitably links me

to a tender, yet willing, vulnerability. It softens, sharpens and energizes my relationship to life and begins to involve the heart in the wholeness of practice. In particular, I can be more compassionate to all those I see who are still fearful of opening to the fullness and abundance of life: I witness, through them, how the darkness of fear and separateness obscures and obstructs all our attempts to move towards a sense of deeper connection. I become the pupil and they the teachers of what it is to be human."

(Hugh said that, although "being gentle" might sound mundanely simple, it represented the first steps of an incredibly profound practice. Gentleness, in effect, is the defiance of our own will. If I can hold back, just for a second, from acting automatically in whatever I do and see, think and feel, and, instead, allow myself to question whether I could bring a more gentle energy to this, then I am, in effect, creating a sacred interruption that allows a moment's space for a stronger Will to be felt in me, rather than submitting to a will of my own.

(To evoke gentleness in me creates a "still point" in between any impulse that arises in me, and the completely mechanical response that inevitably follows it. For a very brief moment, I am still; not pushing forward, heedlessly, with what my self wants. Freed from the constant drama of restlessness and anxiety, I can experience a moment of life from a truer place in myself. I have more presence and more time and space and choice in how I act. With less distraction and contraction, another quality of energy is free to become creative – to live more expansively within me. In that one miraculous second of freedom, I come closer to serving God.)

"Through the mirror of our daily life we can begin, right now, to notice when we are caught in the grip of our desires and tensions and are not gentle; when we judge; when something harsh enters into our response or reaction to the external and internal happenings that reach our awareness…and, to some extent, we can free ourselves from them. We can breathe gently into our body. We can slow down and become quieter. As we move towards stillness, we see what in us is not still and we can bring gentleness as a response to that, too."

Hugh stressed, again and again, as he talked, the importance of understanding that the effects of this practice stretch far beyond our own lives: gentleness is not just for me. Its impact can influence all of us, here on earth, *as it is in heaven.*

"Though gentleness, in a very real sense, turns us towards the Divine, by doing so, it also allows us to engage more fully in the world from deeper within ourselves.

"All the problems that trouble us in the world exist because we do not have an open, unashamed relationship with our selves. As a result, it is impossible for us to be in proper relationship to each other, to life and to the planet, which hosts us. My God also becomes punishing.

"Accepting the simplicity of this inner practice allows us to meet the unconscious 'shadow' aspects of our life in surrender and acceptance …but, in this case, surrender is not submission but an opening to something greater than myself; and acceptance is not approval but a letting go of the fear that accompanies '*I don't want it to be like this!'* into a greater, freer trusting in how things are.

"By moving towards the world with the intention to be gentle, we begin to break the fortress walls of our separateness and self-defending. When we are gentler and more loving towards our self (especially to those aspects of us that we judge as 'bad'), we are freed from the persecution of judging others. So gentleness becomes, of itself, a deeply powerful spiritual practice that allows us to link here, in this very moment – however briefly or distantly - to a living experience of Christ's love.

"To become meek in the way we talk, act and treat our self, and others, brings with it a joy of being in an ever-deepening relationship, both with our own life and with a greater, more essential world. We become more open and more permeable to the enervating, revitalizing and renewing power of Divine Life.

"By becoming openly receptive to the sacredness of both life and my own purpose in it, I am able to come into relationship with the rest of the world in a way that honors the holiness in all things. This, quite literally, is the heart of Christian fellowship."

(The following day, Hugh offered me a specific exercise –something, he said, that would place my feet upon the Way and was safe for me to practice by myself.

Later on he was to share much more but, for the time being, these are the instructions he revealed. He called it "breathing into the Lord's Prayer". It was an exercise, he said, that teaches us some of the obstacles that arise when we give ourselves an inner task.

*The exercise, itself, offers us a way to begin to observe the mind and to practice placing our attention. Hugh said it was meant to be both a search and a service. When I asked him what he meant by 'service', he said that the meaning of the Lord's Prayer has become lost to most of us. We could help by guarding against the danger of voicing the words mechanically, and, instead, **feel** into some sense of their true meaning.*

Here are the instructions he gave me:

• *Relax. (You will need to be sensible about creating the conditions for this. Find a quiet place where you are not going to be disturbed. This exercise can be as short as five minutes or it can be repeated and expanded into a longer period of time. Your clothes should be loose-fitting and you should feel warm and comfortable. Find a tense-free way of sitting. A chair, stool or cushion is fine. The important thing is that your back is straight and your knees are not higher than your pelvis. Place your hands on your lap so that your shoulders can relax and your chest expands freely. Your head should be straight and your chin tucked in slightly to elongate the neck at the base of the skull).*

• *Close your eyes. Allow your body and your mind to quieten into the simplicity of this practice. Just notice how your breathing settles and accepts the silence. Give it time. You will notice, in this new state, that you are no longer being lived by your anxieties in quite the same way. A sense of the sacred is closer and with it can come a feeling of gratitude for this very simple transformation. As you become more relaxed, silently bring the words of the Lord's Prayer to mind, phrase by phrase, each time you exhale.* **(Our father/ which art in heaven/ hallowed be thy name).**

• *When you breathe out, in prayer, let go of any tightness or tension. Feel the quality of softness in your body as you exhale. Allow your breathing to be natural. Let yourself be breathed in and breathed out. Don't try and change or control things in any way. After each exhalation you may notice an almost imperceptible pause before the inhalation. There is a pure stillness in that moment: breathe that in, as you allow each inhalation to infuse your whole body.* **(Thy kingdom come/ Thy will be done/ in earth/ as it is in heaven).**

• *Notice your thoughts. Let them pass by, as you breathe out. Accept their coming and their going without interest. You are not them. Allow your breath to carry you into the prayer. Let your breathing find each line for itself. The breath symbolizes the sacred movement of Life, of evolution and involution that is God's Will. Notice what gets in the way of that instinctive motion of free expansion and retraction. Don't try to push too many words into one exhalation: wait for the next out-breath to complete it. You* can take as many exhalations as you wish to breathe each line. Avoid any feeling of the words being rushed. Let them resonate in as much space as possible. You might also notice the inhalation lengthening to collect more breath in anticipation of the next part of the prayer being breathed. Again, just notice that and do nothing. Let any judgement go.   **(Give us this day/ our daily bread).**

• *It may well be that you lose your place. If you do, just go back to the beginning and start again.   When your attention is distracted for any length of time and becomes lost to you, notice that with gentleness and let it return to rest again on your breath. You can repeat each line, as you wish. Try, though, to complete the full prayer at least once by the end of the practice.* **(Forgive us our trespasses/ as we forgive those/ who trespass against us).**

• *Resting in the words of the prayer will help subdue the inter-ference of the process of thinking. When you witness the presence of stillness and silence in your breath and body, more subtle witnessing thoughts may arise, such as "I can do this!" or "I want this feeling!" and your attention will once again be led away. Accept this and allow your awareness, gently, to be returned to the words and the breath.* **(And lead us/ not into temptation/ but deliver us from evil).**

• *Leave behind the tension and stress of your life and enter this place of silent meditation and prayer. Try it for short but regular periods of time every day. At the completion of the prayer, spend time just sitting in the silence. Allow your body to accept stillness. This stillness is always there. It is eternal.* **(For thine is the kingdom/ and the power/ and the glory/ for ever and ever/ Amen).**

"God's mercy is to be found in the inner movements of opening and releasing; in the letting go of tensions and strivings. It is a gathering in of a certain kind of attention that expands awareness where, usually, we are distracted or drawn away by thoughts, emotions, sensations or external attractions. This gathering of attention opens me to the deep behavior of Life and to a new sense of harmony and inner order from which can come a radiance of action and a calm force of gesture.

"Can there be more gentleness here? If we let this question become the daily foundation of our Christian practice, it will bring us the power and the strength of 'no force'. To be meek summons the spirit of Jesus into the present. I become open to the holiness of my life.

"The invitation to prayer; to experience the Divine in all things, is there in every moment. The gift of holiness is to be discovered in every action and every movement of our lives and it is unlocked by gentleness. It holds within it the everlasting faith of Christ and is the sacred, active vitality, which animates all his teachings, in the Christian heart.

"Gentleness is the first unfolding of Christian practice, like the bud of a new rose, within which is held all the beauty and perfection of the flower itself. Each movement towards gentleness embodies its own profoundly significant holy flowering."

CHAPTER XIV

The Sacred Longing

The beatitudes are a call to begin. The holy teachings of Jesus of Nazareth that lie behind them bring Christian practice alive with sincerity and compassion and the courage to face our selves anew.

Certainly, my two weeks with Hugh and Peter changed my life...and continues to do so. I try, as often as I can, every day to bring the teachings of the beatitudes into my ordinary life.

I begin to see that to be human is the greatest of all God's journeys. All paths to Him lead through the door of our willing suffering. The suffering of Jesus, Hugh once said, is to know our pain; to see how we cut ourselves off from the ocean of life to which we belong and how we wander, lost, far and wide in search of Him, when he is here, inside us.

The epic life of every single human heart exposes it to fear, violence, conflict, confusion, anger, shame, jealousy, greed, isolation and despair. The path of our lives also leads us to love, joy, shared laughter and sorrow and the deep fulfillment of communion with others. Through it all, often unseen even by ourselves, amidst all our suffering and blindness, we live the sacred longing for Love. For this reason, our arrival at the gates of Heaven is heralded above all else.

Hugh and I meet more often now. Peter has made a full recovery and now leads the work undertaken by the other members of the community in different parts of the world.

He is not the same. How could he be, having been touched by so high a consciousness? Only his own essential being is left and, according to Hugh, Divine Love lives through him without the defilement of the self. There is still a Peter but one who serves and wishes only what God wills.

Shortly before this book was finished, I received a letter from him and I asked his permission to include it. Here it is.

The beatitudes lead us to the transformative, healing nature of Divine Love. Love opens us to eternity; Love attracts and draws us towards each other; Love calms the mind's fear and allows attention to be gathered back inside our bodies in search of God; Love cultivates caring and giving and a lucid serenity, amidst all the contractions and tensions of life.

Love destroys the wish for power; Love links us to the unity of the Infinite; Love changes all it touches yet Love itself cannot be changed.

We are all part of the greatness of Love. Lord grant us moments when we can know its presence in us and in all that lives, in all actions and in all the beauty and harmony of mother earth. We are alive because of Love. Love is in us, waiting to heal us when we are motherless and fatherless, friendless and alone. The blessedness of God's Love within us binds us and attracts all living things to each other.

We are called by each of the beatitudes to give ourselves to the mystery of God. The vastness of what we do not know is the Infinite Vastness to which we belong, heart and soul. The highest knowledge is in oneself yet we have to accept that we cannot immediately do what is asked of us as Christians. We must believe in Divine Presence but we must also put it to the test.

The Christian path opens the heart and mind to a new knowledge and a new way of living. All kinds of teaching can inspire us but inspiration does not, by itself, lead us to God.

We must learn to feel the whole of Christ's journey within ourselves. All of that must become part of our own experience, as we move towards God, once again, by living the beatitudes in the heart of our lives.

Nothing that belongs to the material world defines who I am. Why hold on to anything that comes and goes? However hard I might strain to possess even a single breath, I have to let it go. All that I have that is "mine" is my refusal of God's Will – a will that will be done, despite me. However often I turn away from God's door, His holy rejoicing always greets my return.

And so I try, again and again. I wish to submit to a living crucifixion when the inner experience of but one drop of Christ's suffering grants me a moment of being free.

I offer my self to God. I begin with a prayer. I make the words myself. They say: "Yes! I am willing. Lord have Mercy!"

I realize they are not my words at all.

BOOKS

O is a symbol of the world, of oneness and unity. In different cultures it also means the "eye", symbolizing knowledge and insight. We aim to publish books that are accessible, constructive and that challenge accepted opinion, both that of academia and the "moral majority".

Our books are available in all good English language bookstores worldwide. If you don't see the book on the shelves ask the bookstore to order it for you, quoting the ISBN number and title. Alternatively you can order online (all major online retail sites carry our titles) or contact the distributor in the relevant country, listed on the copyright page.

See our website www.o-books.net for a full list of over 400 titles, growing by 100 a year.

And tune in to myspiritradio.com for our book review radio show, hosted by June-Elleni Laine, where you can listen to the authors discussing their books.

MySpiritRadio

SOME RECENT O BOOKS

Who on EARTH was JESUS?
the modern quest for the Jesus of history
David Boulton

What happens when the Christ of faith meets the Jesus of history? This is the question that preoccupies Boulton in an amazingly good synthesis of historical Jesus scholarship. His scope is as wide-ranging as it is even-handed; from theologians to scholars to popes, he distills their thoughts into a comprehensible and comprehensive survey of the best of the contemporary thinkers. Readers will find no overt proselytizing in this book. Instead, the author treats them to an unbiased look at the ever-changing discipline of Jesus studies. In the end, Boulton understands that it is not the scholar, nor the theologian, who will define the kingdom on Earth. Rather, it will be the job of all of us to discern the Jesus of today from words written long ago. This book is not to be missed.
Publisher's Weekly
9781846940187 448pp £14.99 $29.95

Introduction to Radical Theology
Trevor Greenfield

Trevor Greenfield depicts the landscape of radical theology with a pleasing balance of broad stroke and fine detail. His book will engage and benefit the college student and armchair reader alike.
Anthony Freeman, author of *God In Us*
1905047606 208pp £12.99 $29.95

Breaking Free
Christopher Power

Anyone who thinks they will never be able to break free of the misery which engulfs them should read this book. From an unfortunate beginning Christopher Lee Powers' life degenerated into chaos. Today he has a life many would envy. Reading how he did it made me realise what a human spirit can accomplish when it tries. **Denise Robertson** ITV "This Morning"

"An inspiring and uplifting story". **Susan Beresford** Actor and Voice Coach
978-1-84694-171-9 112pp **£7.99 $16.95**

The First English Prayer Book (Adapted for Modern Use)
The first worship edition since the original publication in 1549
Robert Van de Weyer
This new edition of the 1549 first Prayer Book presents Cranmer's services in a form which is practical, accessible and easy to follow. delightful... excellent resource... I recommend this book to anyone interested in liturgy or in the history of the Anglican tradition.
The Rev. Jim Snell, *The San Joaquin Star*
9781846941306 160pp **£9.99 $19.95**

Who Is Right About God?
Thinking Through Christian Attitudes in a World of Many Faiths
Duncan Raynor
This book is both important and readable, because it has been forged in the daily "real time" interplay between the issues and views that it discusses, and because it is given rigour and intellectual coherence by the gifted author, who has an Oxford training in philosophy, as well as theology.
The Very Revd Robert Grimley, Dean of Bristol Cathedral
9781846941030 144pp **£11.99 $24.95**